SISTERS AND SAINTS

SISTERS AND SAINTS

Women and American Religion

ANN BRAUDE

UNIVERSITY PRESS

2008

OXFORD
UNIVERSITY PRESS

Oxford University Press, Inc., publishes works that further
Oxford University's objective of excellence
in research, scholarship, and education.

Oxford   New York
Auckland   Cape Town   Dar es Salaam   Hong Kong   Karachi
Kuala Lumpur   Madrid   Melbourne   Mexico City   Nairobi
New Delhi   Shanghai   Taipei   Toronto

With offices in
Argentina   Austria   Brazil   Chile   Czech Republic   France   Greece
Guatemala   Hungary   Italy   Japan   Poland   Portugal   Singapore
South Korea   Switzerland   Thailand   Turkey   Ukraine   Vietnam

First published in hardcover as *Women and American Religion* (2000).

Published by Oxford University Press, Inc.
198 Madison Avenue, New York, New York 10016

www.oup.com

Oxford is a registered trademark of Oxford University Press

Library of Congress Cataloging-in-Publication Data
Braude, Ann.
Sisters and Saints: women and American religion / Ann Braude.
     p. cm.
Includes bibliographical references and index.
ISBN 978-0-19-533309-1 (pbk.)
1. Women and religion—United States—History. 2. United
States—Religion. I. Title.
BL458.B67 2007
200.82'0973—dc22   2007026765

Frontispiece: Herminia Villaescusa holds a candle, a missal, a rosary, and white
flowers in honor of the Virgin for her First Communion in a Mexican Catholic
church in 1932. In many communities young girls are still dressed like brides
for their first participation in the sacrament.

9 8 7 6 5 4 3 2 1

Printed in the United States of America
on acid-free paper

For my grandmother, Vicci Sperry

CONTENTS

"Women Are the Backbone of the Church"

An old saying among members of African-American churches can be applied to most religious groups in the United States: "Women are the backbone of the church." The saying has a double meaning. Women provide essential support for the church and affirm its moral role, but their work happens in the background and their support is invisible. It is the men who play the leading roles in religious organizations. As a result, most people assume that women have had little importance in U.S. religious history. Few groups had women as leaders before the 1970s, and the largest ones still do not. Men administered the sacraments, wrote the prayer books, preached the sermons, and made the decisions.

Throughout American history, however, women have been the majority of members in almost all religious groups. There could be no lone man in the pulpit without the mass of women who fill the pews. Women raised money for churches, synagogues, temples, and mosques through bake sales, community suppers, and sewing circles. They embroidered altar cloths, taught Sunday school, prepared festival meals, played the organ, and directed the choir. Perhaps most important, they took their children to their places of worship and educated them in their beliefs. Without such women, there would be no next generation to sustain the faith. And without their material and financial support, there would be no churches, synagogues, or mosques for men to administer. There would be no clergy, no seminaries to train them, no theology to teach them, no denominations to ordain them, and no ceremonies for them to lead unless women found it worth their while to support religious organizations. But no matter how great their contributions, women have usually been asked to take a backseat to male religious leaders.

Why have women been so devoted to religion even though they have been barred from public leadership? Women throughout the centuries have testified that they find strength in religious faith to help them survive extraordinary hardship as well as everyday difficulties. In the past, struggling to hold families together through slavery, immigration, poverty, or personal tragedy, women often felt they received help from God and from religious communities when they could get it nowhere else. As they buried infant children, sometimes one after another, they relied on religious faith for the power to endure what would otherwise be unendurable. And when all went well, the religious significance of baptisms, bar mitzrahs, confirmations, and weddings magnified their joy. Trying to make sense of their lives, women looked to religion as a source of both community and personal identity.

Although religion restricted women's roles in some ways, it expanded them in others. Basing their arguments on religious values, women fought for an enlarged role in society in the nineteenth and twentieth centuries. Women who broke accepted rules about their roles often did so because they believed God wanted them to. "What is impossible for woman when the love of Jesus fills her soul?" asked a Methodist woman in 1859. The power of spiritual experiences emboldened women to seek social as well as religious emancipation.

Religious beliefs have affected every aspect of women's and men's roles in society. Legal codes, educational policies, family structures, and personal relationships have all reflected beliefs about how God wanted society to be ordered. For the first century and a half after the founding of the United States, for example, Americans believed that women did not need to vote because God had placed a husband at the head of the family as a guide and protector. Because of men's God-given role, their votes represented the interests of their wives and daughters. When women began to fight for the vote, they claimed that they should be able to do so because of the moral qualities God had given them as guardians of the home. Religious arguments have been used on both sides of most debates about women's rights, duties, and nature. Women's role in religion has both mirrored and provided the model for women's role in the rest of society.

Because women have played such a central, but often over-looked, role in American religion, understanding their experience is crucial to an understanding of our country's religious history. Likewise, if we want to understand the history of American women, we need to examine the religious beliefs and activities that so many have found so meaningful.

CHAPTER I

Planting Religious Households

W hen Margaret Winthrop was pregnant with her fifth child in 1629, her husband, John, left England to lead a party of settlers to a distant and unknown place: North America. Margaret shared her husband's passion for the new religious movement of Puritanism, so-called because its followers hoped to purify the Church of England of any remnants of Catholicism. As Puritans the couple applauded the Protestant Reformation, which condemned the Catholic Church as mired in worldliness and ritualism. Neither priest nor people understood the meaning of the Latin mass, reformers claimed, and monetary contributions to the church had replaced personal piety. Henry VIII brought England into the Protestant Reformation when he rejected the Pope's authority in order to divorce Catherine of Aragon. But Puritans believed the Church of England had not moved far enough from the hierarchy and rituals of the Catholic Church.

Margaret also shared John's dream of establishing a new society based solely on the will of God. But her pregnancy and that of her daughter-in-law required that they stay behind while their husbands made the risky voyage across the Atlantic. While John Winthrop became the first governor of the Massachusetts Bay Colony, Margaret bore a baby girl named Anne thousands of miles away.

Margaret and John agreed to think of each other every Monday and Friday from five to six o'clock. Their marriage, they believed, was part of God's order among his creatures. As Protestants, they rejected the Catholic Church's belief that celibacy is the highest spiritual state. Instead, they saw marriage as the most godly state for adults. Their God was a God of order. The world he made to reflect his glory embodied his nature in the orderly relations among its inhabitants. God made the world to serve humankind, but he made humanity to serve him. Family, church, and state, in that order, were the instruments he provided to govern relations among human beings. These institutions served to educate human beings and shape them to the will of God. Margaret Winthrop knew that the purpose of her marriage, and of the affection between herself and her husband, was to establish such a family for the promotion of God's order on earth.

In 1631, Margaret Winthrop joined her husband in Massachusetts, where she resumed the role she had played in the Winthrop household in England. As helpmate to her husband, and, with him, head of a large household of children and servants, she had substantial responsibilities. When her husband was away, she took charge. Even when he was at home, she was responsible for feeding and clothing everyone who lived under their roof. She viewed her household labor, as well as her role as a mother, as part of her religious calling to establish God's will on earth. Even her love for her husband was inextricable from her other duties to God, and she accepted her husband's authority over her as part of her marriage and part of God's will. "Best love and all due respect...which my pen cannot express or my tongue utter, but I will endeavor to show it as well as I can to thee, and to all that love thee," Margaret wrote to John while he was away on business. She signed her letter, as always, "your faythful and obedient wife Margaret Winthrop."

Accepting the biblical story that God created Eve from Adam's rib to be his "helpmate," Puritans believed that women were made ultimately for God but immediately for men. "He for God only, she for God in him," wrote the Puritan poet John Milton. The Christian tradition in their view affirmed the subordination of wives to husbands. "Wives be subject to your husbands, as to the Lord. For the husband is the head of the wife as Christ is the head of the church," taught the Apostle Paul, and Margaret Winthrop accepted this idea without question. But John Winthrop also followed Saint Paul's advice: "Husbands, love your wives as Christ loved the church" (Ephesians 5:22–23, 25). He loved his wife ardently, but both took care to remember that their love for each other must always come second to their love for God. "My sweet spouse, let us delight in the love of eache other as the chiefe of all earthly comforts," John wrote to Margaret. He believed that even greater comforts wait beyond this world, where the righteous would enjoy God's glory forever. Their marriage would last only as long as they lived, but the relationship of their souls to God would endure for eternity.

The well-ordered family established by marriage perfectly mirrored the divine plan and allowed for the best possible spiritual environment for its inhabitants. The Puritans placed so much faith in the family as an agent of godly living that they required all members of their settlement to reside in one. Single adults were prohibited by law from living alone. Servants, a category that included skilled artisans as well as household and agricultural workers, lived in the households of their employers, under their spiritual guidance. Under the government of their parents, Puritan children learned the correct relationship to all figures of authority from the Fifth Commandment: Honor thy father and thy mother. They were taught to answer the question "Who are here meant by Father and Mother?" with the memorized statement "All our superiors, whether in Family, School, Church and Common-wealth."

The family was the model for all right relations in society, in which inferiors were connected to superiors in a chain leading ultimately to God. As God ruled over all, husband ruled over wife, parent over child, master over servant, ministers and elders over congregations, and rulers over subjects. These relations were enshrined in law. A wife's submission to her husband included, for example, the relinquishment of all her property to him at marriage. But the status of women in Puritan New England was relatively high in comparison to other societies of the day. Husbands were forbidden to strike their wives or to command them to do anything contrary to the laws of God. In the government of the household, the wife's authority equaled her husband's as a parent of children or as a mistress of servants.

Even more important than the legal rights women gained in the new settlement was the assurance of righteousness they felt as part of a religious commonwealth. Puritan settlers hoped to establish a pure and godly church in New England by limiting church membership to those whom God had singled out for salvation. These "elect" individuals, they believed, experience a dramatic conversion, an internal transformation in which the power of God's redeeming grace cleansed their souls. The elect were predestined by God to dwell with him in heaven. The rest of the population would spend eternity burning in the flames of hell. All New England residents were required by law to attend church. But to become a voting church member, a Puritan had to give a convincing account of this conversion experience. The spiritual authority women felt as a result of conversion was more empowering than any legal change in their status.

It soon became clear that there were more godly women than godly men in New England. From the early days of the commonwealth, the membership records of New England churches show that more women than men could report the experience of God's redeeming grace. This created an unprecedented situation that would help make women the majority in most churches throughout American history.

Why would God set men over women to guide and protect them and then choose more women than men to have wills perfectly attuned to his? Perhaps the experience of submitting to a husband was itself an aid to piety. A 1709 wedding sermon advised women that "Men can learn to command, and rule fast enough, which as Husbands they ought to do, but tis very rare to find that women learn so fast to Submit and obey, which as Wives they ought to." Submission was a discipline, and one that could have spiritual benefits.

The Boston Puritan minister Cotton Mather thought there were more godly women than men because women faced death in childbirth. Bearing children, Mather wrote, turned women's thoughts "toward the Gates of Death, by which We all receive life." Indeed, one in five colonial women died in childbirth. Because women attended each other's childbirths, most had witnessed such a death, and probably more than one. Every expectant mother wondered if she would be next. As the day of her delivery approached, a pregnant woman made two types of preparations. She prepared fresh linens for herself and her child and arranged for a midwife and other female attendants. She also prepared herself spiritually to die, searching her soul to root out any resistance to the will of God. This experience, Mather wrote, increased women's appreciation of the comforts offered by faith in Christ, who promised everlasting life.

Margaret Winthrop prepared herself for death eight times as she prepared for the birth of eight babies. She survived each time, but her children did not fare as well. She buried half of her eight children, including the little girl for whose birth she had stayed behind in England. The baby Anne died on the voyage to Massachusetts and was buried at sea without ever seeing her father. Each time Margaret Winthrop lost a child, she struggled to accept the death as the will of God. And each time, she succeeded. When she died at the age of fifty-six, her husband described her as "a woman of singular virtue, prudence, modesty and piety, and especially beloved and honored of all the country." This was the model woman of Puritan New England, strong in faith and self-discipline, leader of her family, and submissive to her husband and to God.

Not every woman among the British settlers lived up to the Puritan ideal. And not all were as lucky as Margaret Winthrop, who counted a loving husband, a prosperous household, and the respect of the commonwealth among God's blessings. New Englanders had a name for a woman who was dissatisfied with her situation, who got angry when she was mistreated by her neighbors, or who lacked proper respect for the magistrates. They called her a witch.

A witch, according to the Christian thought of the day, was a human being with superhuman powers. Witches received their power from the devil, who demanded their allegiance in return. They had the power to cause illness or death. People, plants, or animals might fall victim to a witch's malice. Witches were blamed for preventing women from conceiving children and for causing miscarriages and birth defects. They were

9

accused of visiting men while they slept and biting, choking, or smothering them.

Witchcraft was a crime punishable by death in both old and New England. Those who emigrated to the Puritan settlement were accustomed to the hanging of witches. They expected the devil to seek followers who would try to undermine their holy experiment. New Englanders accused at least 344 people of witchcraft between 1620 and 1725. Of these, fifty-two were convicted and thirty-five were executed. None of these people claimed to be a witch. Instead they were accused of witchcraft by others, usually people they knew or with whom they had some sort of conflict. One never knew when an angry encounter with a neighbor might result in an accusation. But certain types of people were more likely to be accused, tried, and convicted of witchcraft.

Three-fourths of those accused of witchcraft in New England were women. Half of the accused men were suspected as a result of their association with female witches. Once accused, women were far more likely than men to be tried, convicted, and executed. Why did Puritans find it so much easier to believe that a woman would make a pact with the devil and harm her neighbors than that a man would?

Christian thought traced women's affinity for witchcraft back to the first human sin: Eve's disobedience to God in the Garden of Eden. God created Eve as a helpmate for Adam, and virtuous women like Margaret Winthrop followed this example. But Eve left another legacy, establishing a tendency toward evil in the generations of human women who followed her. According to the biblical account, Adam and Eve lived in the Garden of Eden, in perfect harmony with the will of their creator. God told them they could eat the fruit of any tree in the garden except one, the Tree of Knowledge. But Eve, tempted by the devil, who had assumed the form of a serpent, ate from that forbidden tree and offered its fruit to Adam. As a result of this first human act of disobedience to God, Adam and Eve fell from the state of purity and innocence in which they were created. God decreed that women would bring forth children in pain and suffering. Since then, in the Christian view, all human beings are born in need of redemption because they inherit a sinful nature from their first parents. This made women responsible for all human suffering. Sin, death, want, and affliction all resulted from woman's role as a temptress. A good woman was a blessing for which any man should be grateful, but a bad one might be a witch who should be hunted down and killed.

In Europe clergymen used a book called the *Malleus Maleficarum* (The Hammer of Witches) to help identify witches. Written by two German churchmen in 1468, the *Malleus* stated, "More women than men are ministers of the devil." Women, the authors explained, were created intellectually, physically, and morally inferior to men. They were subject to uncontrollable desires and were dissatisfied with their deficient abilities. Unable to control their appetites and angry at their inferiority, women were likely to turn to the devil for help in gaining power.

In Catholic Europe the image of Eve as sinner stood in contrast to the image of the Virgin Mary, the mother of Christ, model of obedience and godly womanhood. Catholic women could follow Mary's example by becoming mothers willing to make any sacrifice for their children or by becoming nuns, whose vow of celibacy emulated Mary's virginity. Protestant Reformers downplayed the role of Mary, along with all the saints who Catholics viewed as intercessors between humans and God. This left the role of helpmate as the only ideal of Christian womanhood available. To fulfill this role, a woman needed a husband to

11

help and obey. Some women in New England found themselves unable to meet these expectations.

Katherine Harrison was one such woman. Like many women convicted of witchcraft, she was first accused shortly after her husband's death, which had left her with substantial property. John Harrison died in 1666 with no male heir. He left all his property to his wife and three daughters, making his widow the wealthiest woman in Wethersfield, Connecticut. Unlike most widows in colonial America, Katherine chose not to remarry. For Puritans, this meant that she did not serve the purpose for which God had created her. If she remarried, all of her substantial estate would become the property of her new husband. As a single woman with independent means, Katherine Harrison threatened the order that Puritans believed represented the will of God.

Neighbors began collecting evidence that Katherine Harrison was a witch two years after her husband's death. By that time it was clear that she did not intend to have a prompt second marriage. Even before her marriage, some had suspected Katherine of witchcraft. She could spin more fine linen yarn in an afternoon than any other woman—perhaps this resulted from the devil's assistance. She was also a healer who attended many Wethersfield residents in times of illness. But when she was unable to save a patient, some suspected her of killing instead of curing. None of these neighbors raised their fears publicly, however, until Katherine Harrison became a wealthy widow.

In 1668, Harrison complained to the magistrates that her neighbors were vandalizing her property. Her oxen had been beaten, some livestock killed, and her corn crop had been intentionally trampled by her neighbors' horses. The court gave Harrison no relief. Instead, it tried her for slandering her neighbors, Michael and Ann Griswold. Because the Griswolds were recruiting other witnesses to testify to Harrison's witch-craft, she said that "Michael Griswold would Hang her though he damned a thousand soules," court records reported. As for his own soul, she added, "it was damned long ago." For this, the court fined Harrison £40 and required her to make a public confession of her sins.

When the court rejected Harrison's protest against the unusually large fine, she deeded her property to her daughters, appointing two male relatives as trustees. She then left the colony for Westchester, New York, hoping to start a new life. Her repu-tation as a witch followed her, however. Two new neighbors filed a complaint that she should not be allowed to settle among them because of the suspicions against her in Connecticut. Before any action was taken, her oldest daughter became engaged to the son of Thomas Hunt, who had protested her presence in Westchester. Hunt now became a supporter, and all objections to her residence there were dropped. Once the family property was returned to male control, witchcraft accusations against Katherine Harrison ceased.

Though the actual number of women accused of witchcraft was small, the threat of being accused hung over all women. The message was clear: Do not fight with your neighbors, do not assert your property rights, do not remain outside of a household with a male head. If you feel angry at your treatment, do not say so. Be obedient to civil and religious authorities. Then, you will not be accused of witchcraft. Even more powerful than these external threats were the internal concerns of religious women. Women who wanted to serve God sought to cleanse themselves of any impulses they believed to be contrary to his will. When they saw witchcraft trials and accusations, they saw examples of the type of woman they did not want to be. When they were tempted to rebel against authority or to resent their subservience, they knew this to be the devil's work. Most women in New England agreed with the magistrates in condemning witchcraft and won respect for their roles in well-ordered families.

For two hundred years after the Puritans arrived in New England, British settlement in North America was concentrated in a relatively small area along the Atlantic coast. The rest of the continent was occupied by 10 to 20 million Native Americans, speaking two hundred different languages and living in a variety of different ways. Some areas were controlled by French and Spanish colonial forces.

Indigenous religions affirmed the family structures of their own societies in the same way Puritans related a woman's religious role to her role as wife and mother. In most Native American cultures, the concept of a family or household extended beyond those living together in the same shelter. The family to whom one was obligated by religious duty as well as personal affection might include an entire clan, connected by complicated ties of kinship and marriage. It might also include relatives in the natural world, animals or plants whose spirits were understood to participate in the life of the family or the tribe. On the Great Plains Lakota girls learned to pray for *mitake oyasin*, meaning "all my relations," indicating their broad connections to the human, natural, and spirit worlds. Lakota religious ceremonies encouraged girls to feel a sense of responsibility for their entire tribe, not just for their parents and siblings.

Just as the biblical story of Adam and Eve served as a source of Christian ideas about male and female roles, each American Indian nation looked to its own origin story for ideals of feminine character and family relations. Female figures vary widely from story to story, always reflecting the group's values and way of life. Some traditions emphasize male gods and spirits as the source of life, and others trace tribal origins to female deities.

In many sacred histories both female and male divine figures play a role in the origins of life, each with a distinctive role that sets an example for human women and men.

The Iroquois, one of the largest and most powerful eastern groups, trace their origins to a time when there was no land, only sea and sky. In the sky-world lived divine beings who resembled people. One, a woman, was expecting a child. During her pregnancy she craved all kinds of strange delicacies, and she began to search for them everywhere. She dug at the roots of the Great Tree that grew at the center of the sky-world. She soon dug through the floor of the sky, and saw the sea below. Leaning over to look through the hole, she slipped. Grabbing at the tree's roots, she caught bits of it in her fingers as she fell through the hole.

The birds of the sea saw the woman plunge and flew wingtip to wingtip under her to break her fall. The great sea turtle allowed her to land on its back. Then the muskrat dove to the bottom of the sea to bring up a tiny clump of soil. The woman placed the clump of dirt on the middle of the turtle's back. Then she began to move around it in the direction that the sun goes, the same way Iroquois move in ceremonies today. As she circled, the earth grew until it was big enough for her to plant the roots she brought from the sky-world. Finally, she gave birth to a daughter. Together they kept walking in a circle so that the earth and the plants would continue to grow.

When the daughter came of age, she conceived twin sons. They argued inside her body. The right-handed twin wanted to be born in the normal way. But his brother insisted on being born through his mother's armpit, which killed her. From her body sprang the plants that made Iroquois life possible. From her head grew corn, beans, and squash, known as "the three sisters." From her heart sprang the sacred tobacco, whose smoke carries the people's thanks up to the sky-world. Iroquois women perform ceremonies so that the corn, beans, and squash will grow to feed the people. They call the woman who gave them the three sisters "our mother."

When the twins grew up, they created animals. The right-handed twin made animals that eat plants, and the left-handed twin created animals who feed on prey. The right-handed twin made nuts and berries to feed his creatures. The left-handed twin made poisons and medicines for both good and evil. Finally, the left-handed twin created the Iroquois people, who embody both his own qualities and those of his brother.

Iroquois women traditionally cultivated the crops on which the people depended, while men provided for their families by hunting. Their story of creation shows the divine origins of women's agricultural role. Care for corn, beans, and squash is a woman's responsibility—both to her family and to her faith. The male characters in the origin story create the animals that men hunt for and that figure in their ceremonial activities. Men's and women's roles are complementary. Both men and women have a role in creation, and the activities of both are necessary to the life of the people.

As Native and European cultures clashed, the proper roles of men and women were a serious point of contention. When British settlers saw women take responsibility for agricultural labor, they concluded that native men did not work and therefore did not perform the role God had ordained for men as head of the family. Settlers believed Native Americans needed to be converted to Christianity and hoped that they would adopt English family structures and gender roles. Missionaries were disappointed when some converts accepted faith in Christ without abandoning their own ways of living.

In the British colonies of the American South, as in New England, women found support in Christian faith for their family roles. But southern households were more likely than those in the North to include enslaved Africans. In part because of the institution of slavery, southern Christianity, both black and white, developed distinctive ideals concerning the role of women in the family. Religion had not been the reason for British settlement in the American South as it had in New England. But it would ultimately become central to the culture that evolved there.

Africans brought to North America as slaves were separated from their families and often from anyone else who spoke their language. This made the perpetuation of African religious systems and family structures extremely difficult and often impossible. Although African worship styles and religious beliefs influenced southern Christianity, the religions from which they derived did not survive the treacherous Atlantic passage or the brutal conditions of slavery.

British settlers saw the spread of Christianity as justification both for the subjugation of American Indians and for the importation of African slaves. The British government encouraged Christianization and baptism of slaves, and it sponsored the Society for the Propagation of the Gospel in Foreign Parts to encourage the religious instruction of black, Native, and English inhabitants of the colonies. Slave masters initially resisted allowing the religious instruction of slaves out of concern that they would be required to free those who became church members. This objection was overcome by colonial legislatures, which enacted statutes stating that baptism did not alter an enslaved person's legal status.

Christian slaveholders eventually developed an ethic that encouraged the religious instruction of slaves. If they could show that Christianity and slavery could coexist, it would bolster the moral justification for slavery. Plantation missionaries emphasized the apostle Paul's letter to the Ephesians: "Slaves, be obedient to your masters" (Ephesians 5:6). They hoped that Christianity might make those held in bondage more docile and reliable.

The conflict between the requirements of slavery and Christian teachings about women's roles could not be as easily overcome. Slavery made it impossible for African-American women to follow the moral code they were taught in church. Told to be faithful wives and mothers, they were divided from husbands and children by sale. After separating couples, slaveholders might pair a man or woman with another partner, hoping to profit from their offspring. How could slaves enter into Christian marriages if they were legally barred from marrying at all? Told to be chaste, women slaves were also subject to the sexual whims of their masters.

Southern churches struggled to accommodate church discipline to slavery. Because churches excluded members who had sexual contact outside of marriage, they had to determine when a slave couple was considered to be married. In general, churches regarded as married those couples who "come together in their former and general custom, having no other companion." But what if such a couple were parted by sale—was it adultery if one took another partner while the former spouse was still alive? In 1790 a Baptist church in North Carolina considered the case of "Negro Sam," whose wife had been taken out of the state by her master and married to another man. They decided that "it shall not break fellowship with us if Sam should git another wife."

About the same time, the white decision makers of the Virginia Portsmouth Baptist Association considered the issue of marriage among its enslaved members. "Is it lawful and agreeable to the Word of God, for a black Man servant (or Slave), who has been Married, and his wife removed from him a great distance, without his or her consent to marry another Woman during her Life or not?" After much debate the question was withdrawn. In its place the association considered the issue of whether white members who separated married slaves should be censured by the church. This question also received much debate, but "was thought by a Majority to be so difficult, that no answer could be given it." Church members were admonished not to separate slave couples but, in this church at least, were not punished for doing so.

Those enslaved to Christians could appeal to a shared set of moral values that governed both master and slave. This may account in part for the swift spread of Christianity among the slave community and the tenacity with which many held to their faith. While slaves had no legal rights that whites were bound to respect, they knew that at the final judgment a single standard would apply to all. But what if one's master was not a church member? This could be a problem, especially for women. How could a Christian slave hope to maintain her chastity, for example? A white man's "property" in his slave included nonconsensual sex. He might avail himself of this right, or he might grant it to a male slave. In either case, any offspring became the master's property. The law recognized no crime of rape against black women.

This sexual aspect of slavery conflicted with Christian norms for whites as well as blacks. Plantation mistresses saw the birth of mixed-race babies who resembled their own children. Whether they blamed their husbands or the stereotype of black women's promiscuity, they knew that slavery threatened their own roles as Christian wives. Plantation mistresses began offering religious instruction to slaves as part of their wifely duties, and missionary activity became a passion for many. The evils of slavery, wrote one planter's wife, "are linked by a chain which reaches into the dominion of satan." But, like their northern counterparts, southern wives and mothers viewed their own families as their first priority and sought to provide a model of piety for their husbands and children.

Outside of the South, many religious movements followed the example of the Puritans in attempting to establish societies that would mirror God's order by placing the family at the center of religious life. The Shakers and the Mormons, especially, reveal the close parallels between religious beliefs and family structure.

The Shakers were founded by Ann Lee, an English Quaker who arrived in the British colonies with her husband in 1774. Calling themselves the United Society of Believers in Christ's Second Appearing, the group was known as the Shakers because of the rhythmic dancing that formed part of their weekly worship service. The Shakers viewed the incarnation of God in human form as incomplete because Jesus, a male, represented only half of humankind. God had now completed the incarnation by assuming the form of a human woman, Mother Ann Lee. This meant that the second coming of Christ had, in fact, occurred, and it was time for God's people to live as he said they would when Christ returned. The most distinctive and controversial feature of Shaker life was celibacy. Ann Lee taught that lust, not disobedience, was the original sin that caused humanity's rift with God. By abandoning sexual contact between men and women, her followers, she believed, lived on earth as they would in heaven, where "they neither marry nor are given in marriage." She called on those who would live a godly life to abandon their former ways and join Shaker communities, where members held property in common, worked for the common good, and lived under the spiritual guidance of Shaker elders and eldresses. There Mother Ann admonished her "children" to put their "hands to work and hearts to God." The result was the most successful communal religion in U.S. history. At its height, from 1830 to 1850, about six thousand Shakers lived in nineteen communities across the country.

Celibacy had a clear appeal for some women in an era without birth control. Ann Lee experienced repeated miscarriages and stillbirths before Christ appeared to her and revealed that celibacy was the path to salvation. Life in a Shaker village meant giving up old family relationships, but they were replaced by new ones. Each village was organized into "families," consisting of as many as one hundred people who lived in the same building. Adult Shakers were known as brothers and sisters, and elders were called Mother and Father. Within the family, the division of labor mirrored that in the outside world. Sisters spent long hours spinning and weaving cloth, in addition to routine cooking, cleaning, baking, canning, washing, and ironing. Men cared for crops and livestock and also worked as artisans. Considering their work to be an act of religious devotion, the Shakers became renowned for their inventiveness and for the quality of the products they produced for sale. Americans still admire the classic simplicity of Shaker furniture and architecture.

United by religious bonds, the Shakers promised family relations more satisfying than any other earthly connections. One believer described the Shaker family in Enfield, Connecticut, in 1868: "Here in this lovely valley you will find Fathers and Mothers to caress you as all Mothers know how to, and Brothers and sisters that it fairly makes your heart beat...to even think of parting with those who appear to be much engaged in their efforts to come up into a higher life." Like the Puritans, the Shakers saw the family as the highest expression of God's order among human beings. But the Puritans viewed family bonds as limited to this world, whereas in heaven all souls would focus exclusively on God. The Shakers, in contrast, believed that family organization would persist in heaven. By living in families of fathers, mothers, sisters, and brothers, they hoped to realize heaven on earth.

Another group that believes that families exist in heaven is the Mormons, the Church of Jesus Christ of Latter-day Saints (LDS). Even more than the Shakers, Mormons emphasize the continued distinctive roles of husbands and wives for all eternity. Founded in upstate New York in 1830 by Joseph Smith, Mormonism has become America's largest homegrown religion, with more than five million members in the United States and an equal number in other countries. It also became the basis of one of America's most distinctive regional cultures when Mormons migrated to Utah in 1847, establishing a religious commonwealth distant from any other non-Native settlement.

Joseph Smith and his contemporaries were disturbed by the proliferation of religious outlooks in early nineteenth-century Europe and America. As revivals increased Americans' sense that they needed to be saved, various Christian groups offered competing paths to salvation. With the founding of the LDS, Smith proclaimed, God had restored the priesthood that had been disrupted by the corruption of the Catholic Church and by the dizzying array of Protestant denominations. Choosing Smith as his prophet, God had restored direct communication with his people, settling once and for all the question of religious authority.

Just as Smith was concerned about reestablishing an unquestionable source of religious authority, he also wanted to restore a single source of authority in the family: the father. For Mormons these two ideas are inseparable. Mormon theology depicts God as a flesh-and-blood patriarch, rather than the unlimited, unknowable deity of Christian and Jewish tradition. This fully embodied view of God suggests the core belief of Mormonism: that all men can progress toward godhood. "As man is, God once was: as God is, man may become" was one early Mormon's summary of his beliefs. This flesh-and-blood God, not surprisingly, has a wife. To become like God, then, every man must be married. The closest women can come to divinity is to marry a man who will himself ultimately become a god and to serve as his wife forever.

Marriage, then, is central to the LDS religious path. In 1841 in the Mormon settlement of Navoo, Illinois, it became the subject of an important revelation. Here Joseph Smith presented a "new and everlasting covenant of marriage" as one of the few sacred ceremonies to be performed only inside a specially constructed temple. According to Smith, ordinary civil marriages joined couples together "for time," that is, for the duration of their lives. The new ceremony consecrating a "celestial marriage," in contrast, would seal the union of husband and wife "for time and eternity." Because Mormonism depicts heaven as a heightening and accentuation of life in this world, it was impossible to imagine it without the greatest of this world's blessings—marriage.

The Mormons' elevation of marriage to a divine law led to their most controversial doctrine: polygamy, or plural marriage. In heaven, men who had been sealed in celestial marriages on earth would be great patriarchs surrounded by their wives and children, served by those who had lacked wives and children on earth. Through the natural increase of the families they founded, these men would eventually rule over whole new worlds, peopled by their descendants of many generations. Polygamy was seen as a more exalted form of celestial marriage. Mormons believed that an infinite number of disembodied souls were waiting to be born as Mormons, hoping someday to advance to heaven. The quickest way to usher the most souls to heaven was for righteous men to have many wives and father many children, all of whom would spend eternity in heaven together.

The LDS made women very important theologically because it considered them necessary to men's salvation. Women's own salvation rested on their status as wives. The role of wife, however, had divine sanction, with God's wife serving as an attainable religious ideal to which all women could aspire. The necessity of marriage for salvation mirrored the economic importance of marriage when Mormons migrated to Utah. Relative to other regions, in Utah wives had a great deal of independence because the frontier settlement depended on their labor. In 1870 Utah Territory became the second U.S. jurisdiction to give women the right to vote (Wyoming preceded it by one year).

The doctrine of polygamy, however, proved so unacceptable to the rest of the country that the U.S. Congress disenfranchised polygamous men in 1882 and all Utah women in 1887. Although Mormons argued that plural marriage was practiced by Old Testament patriarchs and condoned by the Bible, non-Mormons viewed it as an immoral affront to Christian morality. When polygamous husbands were disenfranchised and jailed, their strongest advocates were Mormon women. They defended polygamy as part of the religious freedom established by the Constitution and as a moral alternative to the infidelity practiced by married men who visited prostitutes. Nevertheless, it became clear that Utah Territory would never be admitted as a state until plural marriage was abandoned. In 1890 a new revelation to LDS president Wilford Woodruff accomplished just that, and Utah became a state six years later.

Despite the differences in doctrine, each religious culture that established itself in the United States viewed a specific role in the family as central to a woman's religious duty. From Native American to slave mistress to servant to celibate Shaker sister to Puritan mother to plural wife, each belonged to a group that defined an ideal path to salvation. Each group saw the family as a model of God's order and saw a specific role for women as crucial to the maintenance of the family. In every case, the significance of a woman's role in the family stretched beyond her individual salvation to affect the spiritual fate of her family and her community. Much rested on the piety of women. In the following decades, the importance of women's religious role would become even more evident.

Throughout American history the deaths of children have challenged Christian women to reconcile God's goodness with his greatness. Why would an all-powerful God choose to rip a child from a loving family? The poet Anne Bradstreet, who sailed to New England with John Winthrop, expressed the Puritan view that God takes those we love to remind us that the pleasures of this world are fleeting, and that heaven holds the only hope of lasting happiness. In the same year that her young namesake died, Anne Bradstreet also lost two other grandchildren and her son's wife, who died after giving birth to a premature baby daughter.

In memory of my dear grand-child Anne Bradstreet.
Who deceased June 20. 1669. being three years and seven Moneths old.

With troubled heart & trembling hand I write,
The Heavens have chang'd to sorrow my delight.
How oft with disappointment have I met,
When I on fading things my hope have set?
Experience might 'fore this have made me wife,
To value things according to their price:
Was ever stable joy yet found below?
Or perfect bliss without mixture of woe.
I knew she was but as a withering flour,
That's here to day, perhaps gone in an hour;
Like as a bubble, or the brittle glass,

Or like a shadow turning as it was.
More fool then I to look on that was lent,
As if mine own, when thus impermanent.
Farewel dear child, thou ne'er shall come to me,
But yet a while, and I shall go to thee;
Mean time my throbbing heart's chear'd up with this
Thou with thy Saviour art in endless bliss.

CHAPTER 2

When the Spirit Moves Women

In 1811, Jarena Lee heard a voice saying, "Go preach the Gospel!" She immediately replied aloud, "No one will believe me." But then she heard the same voice say, "Preach the gospel; I will put words in your mouth, and will turn your enemies to become your friends." At first she thought the voice came from Satan in an effort to deceive her. Lee viewed herself as an unlikely choice for a preacher. A twenty-eight year-old free black woman living in Philadelphia, she believed that God could find more effective vehicles to spread his word. But when she prayed to God to know whether the voice was his, she had a vision of a pulpit with a Bible lying on it. This convinced her that the voice came from God and that he had indeed called her to preach, whatever apparent obstacles stood in her way.

When Jarena Lee heard the call from God, she felt an urge that has prompted many American women to challenge previously accepted limitations on their roles. Since the eighteenth century, American Protestantism has been dominated by an evangelical religious style, which encouraged Christians to focus on individual religious experience rather than on the ceremonies of the church. Evangelicals, like the Puritans before them, believed that each person who was saved by God would have a compelling internal conversion experience. But whereas the Puritans believed that only the few elect would experience conversion, by the nineteenth century the new revivalist denominations (like the Methodists) believed that everyone could experience God's grace.

Empowered by the certainty that God worked directly in her own soul, Jarena Lee accepted a view of herself and her potential that the world around her contradicted. The culture of Evangelicalism, and the direct experience of God's power in the conversion experience, propelled many American women into unprecedented roles of public leadership. For African Americans, conversion countered the dehumanizing effects of racism by bolstering a sense of self-worth. They felt that if God valued them enough to sacrifice his son and bestow upon them the gift of everlasting life, he clearly esteemed them more than the nation that bought and sold black people as property. As an African-American woman, Jarena Lee found her identity transformed by God's call.

Lee was a member of Philadelphia's Bethel African Methodist Church, founded in 1793 by African Americans who objected to their second-class status within the city's Methodist churches. Bethel's leader, the Bishop Richard Allen, would go on to found the country's first black denomination, the African Methodist Episcopal Church (AME), part of the evangelical surge that made Methodists and Baptists the largest Protestant denominations in the country. Lee told Bishop Allen that God had called her to preach. He responded that the rules of Methodism "did not call for women preachers."

Lee was relieved. She married and bore two children, putting aside the idea of breaking convention by speaking in public. But after the death of her husband, she once again felt God's call. One day in church, according to her memoir, she spontaneously rose to her feet "by an altogether supernatural impulse" and interrupted the minister's discussion of a biblical text. "God made manifest his power in a manner sufficient to show the world that I was called to labour according to my ability," Lee recalled. Expecting more discouragement from Richard Allen, she was surprised when the bishop rose to his feet to support her. He now believed, he told the congregation, that Jarena Lee was called to preach the gospel as much as any of the male preachers present.

Lee began holding meetings in her home to expound on the Scripture. She became an itinerant preacher, traveling throughout the Middle Atlantic and northeastern states, giving hundreds of sermons each year to black and white audiences. Lee's career followed a pattern that would be repeated by the few exceptional women who became preachers in the denominations most accepting of women's public speaking. She was never licensed as a minister who could take charge of a congregation or vote for denominational officers. But the all-male hierarchy of her church could not deny the power of her spiritual appeals, so they permitted her to become a traveling exhorter, who aroused listeners without threatening the traditional order of the church.

Like other women inspired by the Holy Spirit, Jarena Lee believed that God's call was more important than social conventions and that it revealed a problem with women's limited religious role. "If a man may preach, because the Saviour died for him, why not the woman, seeing he died for her also?" she asked. "Is he not a whole Saviour, instead of a half one, as those who hold it wrong for a woman to preach, would seem to make it appear?" So convinced was Lee that her personal spiritual experience could help bring others to God that she took another unprecedented step for an African-American woman—she wrote and published her autobiography.

Conversion liberated Lee from self-doubt. Her autobiography describes early attempts to commit suicide because of her acute sense of inadequacy and sinfulness. But through the intervention of the Holy Spirit, her despair turned to ecstasy. "So great was the joy," she wrote, "that it is past description." Women like Lee who experienced the direct intervention of God in their lives felt responsible to a higher authority than the church teachings that said they must always defer to their husbands. Religion provided powerful encouragement for women to assume traditional family roles. But it also spurred individual women to abandon those roles under the direct prompting of the Holy Spirit.

From the earliest days of American Protestantism, there are examples of women breaking the rules society set for them because, like Jarena Lee, they believed God required them to do so. Anne Hutchinson, the best-known example, was banished from the Massachusetts Bay Colony because of her religious activism in 1638. Before her religious views were condemned by the men who ran the colony as a threat to church authority, Hutchinson was well known for her piety and intelligence. Governor John Winthrop noted her "ready wit and bold spirit." Her work as a midwife gained her a broad range of acquaintances in Boston. Large crowds assembled in her home to hear her comments on the previous Sunday's sermon and her further thoughts on the religious doctrine presented there.

Hutchinson was a devout woman, dedicated to the Puritan doctrine that salvation could come only as a free gift from God and could not be earned by good works. She believed that behavior in this world, no matter how virtuous, did not provide evidence of one's prospects in the next. Most Puritans expected that those who led moral lives did so because they had experienced conversion and were bound for salvation. Hutchinson, however, denied any connection between one's actions and the state of one's soul. She insisted on a stricter separation of grace and works. She and her followers made distinctions among the ministers of the commonwealth, finding that some were truly saved while others relied on their good deeds rather than divine grace and were therefore damned. Officials worried that Hutchinson's views threatened the authority of the colony's most important leaders: the clergy.

Massachusetts magistrates soon became alarmed by what Anne Hutchinson taught. Her most troublesome idea, Governor Winthrop noted, was that "the person of the Holy Ghost dwells in the justified person." This meant that a person whose conversion experience justified the belief that he or she had been saved had direct access to the will of God. This view threatened the view of the Bible as the sole source of truth. What if an individual received revelations from the Holy Ghost that conflicted with biblical teachings? Hutchinson's beliefs verged on the heresy known as "antinomianism." Derived from Greek and Latin terms meaning "against the law," antinomianism was the belief that a Christian could achieve salvation by faith alone and need not heed the precise teachings of the Bible. Authorities feared that antinomianism would lead to religious anarchy. They worried that if Hutchinson's following continued to grow, the holy commonwealth would be fatally undermined.

Anne Hutchinson was called to answer these charges before the General Court of Massachusetts, presided over by Governor Winthrop. The court had already banished John Wheelright, a minister who agreed with Hutchinson, for his heretical views. Now they charged Hutchinson with breaking two biblical commandments. First, they accused her of disobeying the Fifth Commandment (Honor thy father and thy mother) by entertaining the supporters of John Wheelright in her home. Failing to respect the authority of the state was considered a breach of this commandment. "Put the case, Sir," Hutchinson said to Winthrop, "that I do fear the Lord and my parents, may I not entertain them that fear the Lord because my parents will not give me leave?" With her considerable intellectual abilities, Hutchinson often outwitted the men who tried her.

Next the magistrates charged that the weekly religious meetings at Hutchinson's home violated biblical prohibitions against women speaking in public and against women instructing men. In response she cited two biblical passages (Titus 2:3–5 and Acts 18:26) that permit women of unusual abilities to teach men. "I call them not, but if they come to me I may instruct them," she said. When the court objected that her scriptural examples did not fit her case exactly, she asked sarcastically, "Must I shew my name written therein?"

Hutchinson answered the magistrates' arguments one by one, always providing a biblical text to support her position. But after days of testimony, during which she was imprisoned without adequate food or water, she finally went beyond the bounds of biblical teaching. When the court asked her how she knew that it was God who had revealed these things to her, and not Satan, she replied, "By the voice of his own spirit to my soul." With this statement Hutchinson claimed to have access to a higher authority than the Bible, and this gave the magistrates reason to convict her. She was banished from the colony, exiled to the wilds beyond British settlement. There she and her followers were killed by Native Americans.

The language used by the court suggests that it might have convicted Hutchinson no matter what she said. When the magistrates charged her with breaking the Fifth Commandment, they said she had played the part rather of "a Husband than a Wife, and a Preacher than a Hearer; and a Magistrate than a subject." These were difficult charges for any woman to refute. If God spoke to her, was she not obligated to tell others? But if she followed divine promptings and told others, she would have to answer to human authorities.

Two centuries after Hutchinson's trial, women like Jarena Lee still had to fight an uphill battle to follow where the spirit led. They often, however, received more support than Hutchinson had because of the wave of evangelical fervor sweeping across the country. Religious revivals went on for days and weeks, sometimes with little other business being conducted. In churches and fields on the Kentucky frontier, in the new commercial centers of upstate New York, and eventually throughout the country, Americans flocked to extended meetings that went on for days at a time. Unprecedented numbers of people experienced conversion. Previously, ministers waited patiently for God to pour out his spirit into a community. Now young preachers of a new generation claimed that human beings could make a revival; that if they provided the right conditions, sinners would be saved. They introduced new measures designed to encourage conversions. Revivalists used a direct and informal preaching style, sometimes calling on individuals by name to confess their sins. Those convinced of their sin sat on an "anxious bench" at the front of the church where the entire assembly could watch with them for signs of God's grace.

Several of the new measures involved women. Revivalists held meetings condemned by critics as "promiscuous assemblies" in which men and women sat together, an innovation in Protestant worship. Women were encouraged to recount their experience of conversion, contrary to traditional prohibitions on their speaking in church. In some cases, like that of Jarena Lee, women even became exhorters or preachers. The most significant innovation for women, however, was the idea that it was not enough to experience conversion; conversion must be followed by a commitment to reform both one's personal habits and the society in which one lived. Revivalism spurred the formation of a web of interlocking social reform movements that would change the face of American culture. Missionary societies, temperance societies (which advocated abstinence from the consumption of alcohol), and the movement for the abolition of slavery emerged from the evangelical fervor of the early nineteenth century. These groups were accompanied by a host of smaller ones such as those opposing dueling, opposing tobacco, and promoting vegetarianism. The movement to improve the status of women also arose out of evangelical reform efforts. In short, revivals inspired Americans to take control of both their own religious destiny *and* other people's behavior.

Women gained a special sense of moral authority because of their role in facilitating revivals. Revivals were led and organized by men, but women's societies often provided the support that made them possible. The Women's Missionary Society of Oneida County, for example, funded the first tour of New York State by the master revivalist Charles Grandison Finney. But women's groups provided more than financial support. For twenty years before his massive harvest of souls in 1825 and 1826, the women of Oneida County had been sowing the seeds of piety through prayer circles, mothers' meetings, and missionary efforts.

Although women constituted a majority of converts throughout the revivals, they made up a smaller majority than women usually did in church membership. Thus revivals marked an increase in the proportion of male church members. This increase, however, seems to indicate an increase in women's influence over male family members rather than a decline in women's religious role. Church records show that male revival converts were often led into church by pious wives, mothers, and sisters.

The abolitionist Theodore Dwight Weld recalled the tactics used by his Aunt Clark to cajole male relatives into attending revivals. She asked him to join her for a morning service on the pretense that Charles Finney, whom he despised, was not preaching until the afternoon. Once there, she led him into a pew and followed with several ladies, making his exit impossible. When Finney began to preach and young Theodore attempted escape, Aunt Clark whispered, "You'll break my heart if you go!" Weld remained, was converted, and devoted his life to evangelical reform.

Women had a lot to gain from men's participation in evangelical culture. Legally subject to and economically dependent on husbands and fathers, women were vulnerable to hard-drinking, lazy, or unfaithful men. Men reborn as Christians absorbed the values of Evangelicalism: temperance, thrift, and productivity. Revival supporters pictured men who formerly spent their leisure time drinking with other men now praying with their families instead. Evangelical morality supplied men with a set of values that many believed benefited women.

One reform movement especially symbolized the strength women gained from evangelical Christianity. This was the moral reform movement, aimed at eliminating prostitution. Advocates hoped to reform both the "fallen women" who worked as prostitutes and the men who patronized them. In doing so, they attacked the double standard that condemned the smallest fall from sexual purity in women, but accepted that moral men might patronize prostitutes. Although most Christians assumed that women tempted men to sin, members of moral reform societies portrayed prostitutes as victims of male lust. They published stories of young girls lured into intercourse by false promises of marriage then shunned by respectable society and left with no alternative but prostitution.

In order to attack the double standard, members of moral reform societies stood outside brothels waiting for the patrons to depart. When the men who had visited prostitutes emerged onto the street, the reformers recorded their names. Then they published the names in their magazine. Many people were shocked that respectable ladies would visit such neighborhoods and mix with fallen women, entering brothels to pray and distribute Bibles. This was an extreme measure for women in the 1830s, and the practice indicates the extent to which a religious conversion could change female behavior.

Evangelicalism encouraged many new departures for women because it emphasized the authority of individual religious experience over the institutional authority of the church. Historians have found that women's religious leadership more often results from this type of direct spiritual contact than from the official authorization of religious institutions. Barred from ordination or theological education, women have been denied access to the standard paths to leadership. But women like Anne Hutchinson, Jarena Lee, and the advocates of moral reform found God's encouragement more persuasive than society's discouragement. In fact, a few American religious groups explicitly encouraged direct communication with the spirit and, as a result, sanctioned women's religious leadership. Two such groups are the Quakers and the Spiritualists.

Since their founding in seventeenth-century England, the Society of Friends, known as Quakers, supported the spiritual equality of women. Quaker doctrine taught that the spirit of God lay within each individual—whether man or woman—and that this Inner Light was the primary source of religious truth. When Pennsylvania was founded by the Quaker William Penn in 1682, the group became a significant presence in the middle colonies of British North America.

Quaker religious worship consisted of silent meetings, in which no one spoke until they felt the promptings of the Spirit. Because the Inner Light was thought to dwell in each and every person, any man or woman might speak in a meeting. Quakers believed that biblical prohibitions on women speaking were abolished once a person experienced conversion because the soul was then reborn. This spiritual rebirth restored the equality of men and women that existed before Adam and Eve were expelled from the Garden of Eden. Quakers, as a result, saw no greater propensity for evil in women than in men. The spiritual equality among members of the Society of Friends did not require ordained ministers to be singled out. But some Friends were recognized as lay ministers who might travel to other meetings to share the Spirit's promptings. This group included women as well as men.

Women also played a role in church government. Women's meetings oversaw the discipline of women members and approved marriages among Quakers. Marriage to a non-Quaker was considered grounds for exclusion of the couple and of any family members who attended the wedding. Women's meetings were charged with determining that both parties were free to marry and had acceptable Quaker credentials. "Select" meetings limited to male members decided the most important practical and financial matters, but even select meetings could not overrule women's meetings regarding marriage or membership.

The unusual spiritual freedom of women within the Society of Friends made them early advocates of women's rights. Pioneer advocates of women's rights, including Susan B. Anthony, Lucretia Mott, and Sarah and Angelina Grimké, emerged from

Quaker meetings. All had their first glimpse of sexual equality during religious experiences within the Society of Friends.

By the mid-nineteenth century, some Quakers felt that their church had lost the spiritual freedom that characterized it during its first two centuries. Meetings became more formal, and members were strictly prohibited from involvement with "the world's people." This conflicted with the spiritual promptings some Friends felt to join with non-Quakers in reform activities, especially those aimed at the abolition of slavery. Among these disaffected Quakers, many turned to the new religious movement of Spiritualism.

Spiritualism began in upstate New York in 1848 when two adolescent girls, Kate and Margaret Fox, heard mysterious rappings on the walls and floor of the family farmhouse. They claimed the raps came from the spirit of a dead peddler who had been buried in the basement. Neighbors soon filled the house asking questions that the spirit seemed to be able to answer. Whatever the source of those first raps, they gave rise to a popular movement of Americans intent on making contact with the spirits of the dead. The basis of Spiritualism as a religious faith was the belief that communication with the spirits of the dead provided proof of the immortality of the soul.

Soon people across the country were attending séances, where they hoped to receive messages from departed loved ones with the help of a human medium, who channeled messages from spirits. Deceased toddlers assured their parents that they were happy in heaven, where their growth and education continued. Parents in the world beyond death promised continued affection and concern for surviving children. Deceased statesmen, artists, and scientists offered wisdom and advice from the next world. The spirit of Benjamin Franklin was a frequent communicator; Spiritualists believed his experiments with electricity presaged their own "spiritual telegraph." Firsthand accounts of life after death undercut the need for Christian explanations of the fate of the soul. Spirits universally reported that they were in a pleasant place and that spiritual growth, not judgment, followed death. Spiritualists rejected the idea of original sin, that all humans inherited sin from Adam and Eve. Instead they believed that all human beings were born good. Created in the image of God, they did not need to be saved in order to enjoy eternal life.

At the center of every séance was a medium, who was believed to be specially suited to serve as a conduit between the living and the dead. In an ironic twist, feminine stereotypes of the day suggested that women would be better mediums than men. Women were considered to be naturally passive and prone to suggestion, presenting few obstacles for the spirits who wished to speak through them. Men, in contrast, were thought to be more rational and more organized, qualities that might get in the way of a spirit who wished to control the medium's body. Spiritualists believed that the very traits that qualified men for leadership in other religious groups—education, intelligence, age, and experience—disqualified them to act as mediums. Instead they sought those who lacked these qualities to serve as mediums. The very best medium was often a fourteen-year-old girl—investigators assumed she did not have a strong enough personality to impede an external intelligence.

In addition to communicating messages from the spirits of the dead, mediums known as trance speakers gave public lectures under spirit control. At a time when it was considered both scandalous and unchristian for women to speak in public, about two hundred women made their living as traveling trance speakers. Cora L. V. Hatch was among the best known of these popular figures. Her career as a medium began in 1851, when she was eleven years old. As a teenager, she became famous for her ability to enter a hall in a trance and then deliver a lecture on any topic selected by the audience.

Audiences flocked to hear Hatch. One popular journalist who attended a lecture in New York described her as having "flaxen ringlets falling over her shoulders, movements deliberate and self-possessed, voice calm and deep, and eyes and fingers no way nervous." Observers were as curious about the fact that an eighteen-year-old girl was speaking in public as they were about the claims of a spirit presence. So confident were many Americans that a young woman could not possibly give a public lecture that they took the fact that she did as proof of spirit guidance. "And very curious it was," the journalist wrote, "to see a long haired young woman standing alone in the pulpit, her face turned upwards, her delicate bare arms raised in a clergyman's attitude of devotion, and a church full of people listening attentively while she prayed!"

The eloquence of trance speakers disarmed audiences skeptical both of spirit communication and of women's ability to speak in public. Mediums justified their departure from traditional women's roles with their belief that they were not the ones who did the speaking. Rather, they said, they only served as vehicles for external intelligences who spoke through them. Like Jarena Lee, some trance speakers resisted the spirits' claims, shunning the public role that was thrust upon them. A product of the culture they lived in, many mediums believed it was inappropriate for women to speak in public. But the spirits often empowered women to do things they themselves believed they could not do.

Spiritualists accepted women as religious leaders. Seeing the centrality of women's public speaking to their cause, they also championed women's rights in general. Several early supporters of Spiritualism also participated in the first women's rights convention held at Seneca Falls, New York, in 1848. Spiritualist conventions became hotbeds of women's rights sentiment, often exceeding formal women's conventions in their demands. But becoming a medium had its limits as a path to women's freedom. While mediumship allowed women to speak in public, it did so in a way that emphasized their passive nature. Many women who started out as trance lecturers eventually became public speakers on their own account. A number of mediums became woman suffrage speakers and advocates for other political causes. They needed spirit help to mount the public platform, but once there, they found they could continue unassisted. In fact, they had to abandon their spirit guides and speak for themselves in order to speak with the authority necessary to influence the political realm.

Another new religious movement giving unusual prominence to one woman's spiritual promptings was Christian Science. Its founder, Mary Baker Eddy, had experimented with Spiritualism. She concluded that the strange events occurring in séance rooms were real but that they did not come from spirits. Instead, Eddy attributed the manifestations to the power of the human mind. She agreed with Spiritualists that there was no change at death. But whereas Spiritualists claimed that the body continued to exist after death, Eddy believed that it had never really existed at all. All that really exists, Eddy taught, is Spirit.

Eddy asserted the absolute power of Spirit over matter, of mind over body. She gave the name Christian Science to the resulting principle that thoughts could heal all human suffering, including physical illness. According to her own account, Eddy discovered the principles of Christian Science following a severe fall on the ice in 1866. She found that she could heal herself through the application of mental principles based on stories of healing in the New Testament. She began teaching her new system of healing to classes first in Lynn, Massachusetts, and then in Boston, publishing the first edition of *Science and*

Health, the Christian Science textbook, in 1875. Christian Science recognizes no objective physical reality but only the reality of Spirit—an infinite, all-encompassing principle of goodness, also called God. The physical world and all evidence of evil are projections of what Eddy called Mortal Mind, the opposite of Spirit. Mortal Mind has no ultimate reality because it is created by human thoughts.

This view led to one of Eddy's most controversial tenets—the rejection of conventional medicine in favor of mental healing. The orthodox medicine of the day viewed all women's ailments—erroneously—as resulting from the reproductive system. To a society that believed a woman's anatomy determined her destiny, Eddy made the startling response that the body does not exist. Mental healing could be a benign alternative to dangerous nineteenth-century medical treatments such as bleeding or dosing with opiates or mercury.

Spiritualism and the Society of Friends encouraged all women to act on the promptings of the Spirit, but Christian Science elevated the spiritual voice of one woman above that of all her followers. Mary Baker Eddy founded a well-organized church with her teachings at its center. Instead of sermons, Sunday services included readings from Eddy's *Science and Health* along with biblical texts. The content of Christian Science inspired many other women to explore the power of their own minds, but anyone who added his or her own views to Eddy's was quickly excluded from the church. The highly centralized and tightly structured organization of the Church of Christ, Scientist, have made Eddy's teachings an enduring feature of America's religious landscape.

As the twentieth century opened, another new religious movement gave broad scope to women's spiritual expression. Pentecostal, or "spirit-filled," churches began to attract many Americans.

Pentecostals believe that the Second Coming of Christ is fast approaching and that in these "latter days" Christians can and should experience the gifts of the spirit described in the biblical account of Pentecost, especially the gift of tongues—spontaneous, ecstatic utterances, usually in unknown languages. These involuntary outpourings of the spirit come most frequently from women. Men have formal control of most Pentecostal services and denominations, but women usually dominate religious services in which the direct outpourings of the spirit have free reign. Women's testimonies are the longest and loudest. They can continue long into the night, and the pastor may never even have a chance to give his sermon.

While most spirit-filled churches explicitly favor male leadership, they cannot always prevent women with unusual gifts from rising to prominence. Charismatic women leaders like Alma White and Aimee Semple McPherson have emerged within Pentecostalism. Alma White began her career as an evangelist assisting her husband, a Methodist preacher. Both Methodist objections to her public role and her own sense that her calling required her to do more than assist her husband led her to found an explicitly egalitarian pentecostal church in 1901, first calling it the Methodist Pentecostal Union, and, after 1917, the Pillar of Fire Church, headquartered in New Jersey. She stressed that she advocated the "pure" doctrines of Methodism, which she believed included the ordination of women. White taught that "equal opportunities should be given to both men and women to enter the ministry."

While White's new denomination was inspired by her belief in women's ministry, Aimee Semple McPherson's centered on her flamboyant personality, rather than any distinctive teaching. In 1921 McPherson built Angelus Temple in Los Angeles as the headquarters of her new denomination, the International

Church of the Foursquare Gospel. McPherson had a dramatic preaching style developed during five years leading tent revivals on "gospel tours" across the country. Known for her distinctive white dress and blue cape, she made her religious services entertaining as well as inspiring. From 1923–26 McPherson preached to crowds of five thousand and more every night at Angelus Temple, where audiences enjoyed her dramatized sermons as well as a robed choir, live orchestra, and brass band.

Examples of women assuming religious leadership because of direct spiritual authorization can be found throughout the world. Americans moved by spiritual forces joined medieval Christian mystics, Muslim spirit mediums in Morocco, and shamans in Asia in reporting extraordinary experiences that placed them beyond the control of male religious authority. Whether this made them saints or heretics depended on how their experience was received by the people around them. In the twentieth century women in some denominations gained access to the more regular paths to religious leadership: ordination and education. It is too soon to know whether women in those groups will cease to have the unusual spiritual experiences that have inspired so many women in the past. Still, for women in many religious groups, the authority of an official position remains out of reach, and the authority of a higher spirit continues to be the only way to claim spiritual leadership.

Jarena Lee's autobiography, like most Christian autobiographies, follows the soul's journey from sin to salvation. It also charts her realization of her true place in God's plan. Through a Christian conversion experience, those who had been told that their fate as individuals did not matter to society gained a conviction that it did matter to God. Whether because they were blacks in a world that condoned slavery or because they were women in a world that insisted they remain silent, the conversion experience gave black Christian women a sense of having overcome the world that hindered them. The converted Christian felt sure that her will was perfectly in line with the will of God, whatever other people might say. Lee published this account of her call to preach in 1836.

O how careful ought we to be, lest through our by-laws of church government and discipline, we bring into disrepute even the word of life. For as unseemly as it may appear now-a-days for a woman to preach, it should be remembered that nothing is impossible with God. And why should it be thought impossible, heterodox, or improper, for a woman to preach? seeing the Saviour died for the woman as well as the man.

If a man may preach, because the Saviour died for him, why not the woman? seeing he died for her also. Is he not a whole Saviour, instead of a half one? as those who hold it wrong for a woman to preach, would seem to make it appear.

Did not Mary *first* preach the risen Saviour, and is not the doctrine of the resurrection the very climax of Christianity—hangs not all our hope on this, as argued by St. Paul? Then did not Mary, a woman, preach the gospel? for she preached the resurrection of the crucified Son of God.

But some will say, that Mary did not expound the Scripture; therefore she did not preach, in the proper sense of the term. To this I reply, it may be that the term *preach*, in those primitive times, did not mean exactly what it is now *made* to mean; perhaps it was a great deal more simple then, than it is now:—if it were not, the unlearned fishermen could not have preached the gospel at all, as they had no learning.

To this it may be replied, by those who are determined not to believe that it is right for a woman to preach, that the disciples, though they were fishermen, and ignorant of letters too, were inspired so to do. To which I would reply, that though they were inspired, yet that inspiration did not save them from showing their ignorance of letters, and of man's wisdom; this the multitude soon found out, by listening to the remarks of the envious Jewish priests. If then, to preach the gospel, by the gift of heaven, comes by inspiration solely, is God straitened; must he take the man exclusively? May he not, did he not, and can he not inspire a female to preach the simple story of the birth, life, death, and resurrection of our Lord, and accompany it too, with power to the sinner's heart. As for me, I am fully persuaded that the Lord called me to labour according to what I have received, in his vineyard. If he has not, how could he consistently bear testimony in favour of my poor labours, in awakening and converting sinners?

CHAPTER 3

Mothers and Daughters Maintain the Home

When Harriet Beecher Stowe lost her infant son Charley in a cholera epidemic in 1849, she did not accept his death with the complacency of her Puritan forebears. Most traditional Protestant theology taught that anyone who died without having had a conversion experience was not among the elect and therefore would not enjoy eternal life in heaven. Now Stowe questioned whether a just and loving God could damn an innocent child who died before he was old enough to sin. She poured her grief into a novel that became the best-selling book of the nineteenth century: *Uncle Tom's Cabin*. Published in 1852, *Uncle Tom's Cabin* is remembered for spreading antislavery sentiment on the eve of the Civil War and for the racial stereotypes it employed in the process. "So this is the little lady who caused this great war," Abraham Lincoln said when he met Stowe. But the popularity of Stowe's novel also marks a turning point in U.S. religious history. It is evidence of the broad acceptance of a liberal trend in Protestant theology and of a new view of women as more spiritual than men.

Stowe portrays women as naturally inclined toward religion. Instead of seeing women either as bent toward evil or as equal to men in their propensity toward sin, Stowe presented women as models of virtue who could provide a positive moral influence on husbands, brothers, and sons. In *Uncle Tom's Cabin* the surest path to salvation is the influence of a loving mother. One character described his mother as "a direct embodiment and personification of the New Testament." He explained that she was "all that stood between me and unbelief." Women, according to Stowe and many of her contemporaries, exerted this extraordinary religious influence because they were dominated by the heart, not the head. Because women were more loving than men, they were better able to demonstrate Christ's love. This new focus on Christ as a loving friend rather than on God as a wrathful father became the hallmark of liberal Protestantism after the mid-nineteenth century.

Harriet Beecher Stowe was one of eleven children of the popular evangelist Lyman Beecher. The family was compared to the twelve Apostles because of their prominent role in shaping American Protestantism. Every one of the seven sons entered the ministry. Beecher was disappointed that his brightest child, Harriet Elizabeth, was a girl. If she had been able to bring her intellectual talents to the ministry, he thought they could have done more good for the world. But *Uncle Tom's Cabin*, would reach more people than all his sons' sermons put together. For Stowe a novel was a better way to teach Christianity than a sermon because it portrayed family relations in domestic settings. A novel could depict the core values of her faith more effectively than any theological discourse.

Uncle Tom's Cabin tells the story of Eliza, a slave mother who flees with her little boy rather than see him sold to satisfy her master's debts. Another slave, Uncle Tom, accepts his fate of being sold so that his master's farm can remain intact as a home for all the other residents, slave and free. Taken downriver in chains by a slave trader, Tom is sold to Augustine St. Clare. St. Clare's angelic little girl, Eva, befriends Tom on her deathbed and secures her father's promise to free all his slaves. But St. Clare himself is killed in a fight before the papers are signed, and Tom is sold once again. This time the vicious Simon Legree purchases Tom for his cotton plantation. When two slave women plan an escape rather than submit to Legree's lechery and brutality, Tom refuses to betray them. Legree beats Tom mercilessly. Tom dies a triumphant death, secure in his Christian faith, forgiving Legree for taking his life.

As part of its Christian message, *Uncle Tom's Cabin* shows men and women living in separate moral worlds. In the public sphere of politics and economics, men make decisions based on expediency and rationality. In the private sphere of the home, women rely on sentiment and emotion. The men's world permits slavery because it places pragmatic concerns above feelings. The women's world condemns slavery because mothers cannot condone the sale of other mothers' children, a practice that denies slave children the surest path to salvation. Stowe portrays the domestic sphere as the place where people learn moral lessons and become good Christians and the economic sphere as the place where those moral lessons are challenged or compromised. Even the ministers are busy trying to defend slavery. The book's female characters, dominated by feelings rather than intellect, become the true teachers of Christian faith.

In one memorable scene, Stowe reveals how the woman in the home is the source of salvation. In this scene Eliza and her child are reunited with her husband, George, who also ran away from his slave master when he learned of Eliza's plan. They meet in the home of a Quaker family that serves as a stop on the

Underground Railroad, a secret network operated by those trying to help escaped slaves make their way to freedom in Canada.
Stowe describes the Quaker matron Rachel Halliday preparing
breakfast and ascribes significance to every detail. "Even the
knives and forks had a social clatter as they went onto the table,"
and the "ham had a cheerful and joyous fizzle." Griddle cakes
were transferred to the table just as they gained "the true, exact,
golden-brown tint of perfection." Rachel poured coffee and
passed pancakes with "so much motherliness" that "it seemed to
put a spirit into the food and drink she offered."

Just sitting at Rachel's breakfast table has a religious influence on George. "This indeed was a home,—*home*,—a word
that George had never yet known a meaning for; and a belief in
God, and trust in his providence, began to encircle his heart."
As a slave, George had never had a home of his own or been
served breakfast by his wife. Now, as he ate Rachel Halliday's
perfect pancakes, "atheistic doubts, and fierce despair melted
away before the light of a living Gospel, breathed in living faces,
preached by a thousand unconscious acts of love and good-will."
Housewives like Rachel Halliday, Stowe wrote, are "God's real
priests, whose ordination and anointing are from the Holy Spirit."
Stowe criticized theology as dry intellectualizing that could not
bring souls to God.

Stowe's popular novel presented a powerful image of the
mother as a ministering angel presiding over the domestic
sphere. This idea emerged at a time when the social changes that
came with industrialization were confining women to the home
in greater numbers than before. In the preindustrial world, most
men and women worked with their families on farms, in small-
scale agriculture. Men might be tilling the fields while women
collected eggs for breakfast or did the washing, but all worked close
to each other. With industrialization, men's work increasingly

moved out of the home to factories and offices. As more and more household items, such as cloth, soap, and candles, were produced outside the home, women from prosperous families had more time to devote to "feminine accomplishments," such as embroidery, playing the piano, or religious activity. The separation of men's and women's work encouraged the development of the idea that the sexes were intended by God to occupy separate spheres.

Outside the pages of novels, however, many women never had the choice of remaining at home. Women who worked in the cotton mills of the North or the cotton fields of the South did so out of economic necessity or legal bondage. Whether they lived in boarding houses or in slave quarters, they did not have the option to retreat to the kind of home envisaged by Harriet Beecher Stowe. But the idea that a good woman never departed from the "woman's sphere" became a Christian ideal, as well as a social one. This meant that any woman who ventured into the public realm was considered immoral. From the home, many believed, a woman should minister to her family, inculcating virtue in her children through her loving performance of domestic tasks. But if she ventured beyond her sphere, she abandoned her religious nature and became an immoral influence on her family.

Stowe chose the story of a slave mother threatened with the loss of her child as a metaphor for her own grief following her son's death. "It was at his dying bed and at his grave," Stowe later wrote about Charley, "that I learned what a poor slave mother may feel when her child is torn away from her." Because Stowe could not believe that a good God would damn her blameless baby to eternal suffering, she rejected her father's revival theology in favor of a belief in childhood innocence. A Christian mother nurtured her children's innate moral qualities, and this love, rather than a violent conversion experience, now offered

Christians assurance of God's grace. In trying to reconcile Charley's death with her belief in a loving God, Stowe came to regard the deaths of infants as examples *not* of God's cruelty but of his tender mercy. By taking them early, God preserved the souls of innocent children from the corrupting influence of the world—a world where well-meaning men, for example, might be forced to sell their slaves out of financial necessity. Thus the suffering of survivors became a way to experience God's love. All mothers, like Mary, the mother of Jesus, must willingly sacrifice what they love most.

In *Uncle Tom's Cabin*, the character of Eva, the little girl who convinces her father to free his slaves, embodies the innocence of childhood. Eva loves everybody and convinces them all to do good for her sake, from her slaveholding father to a naughty motherless slave child. Eva has golden curls and a beautiful face "like a kind of psalm that makes one want to be good." She loves to hear Uncle Tom struggle to read the Bible, because he accepts it at face value, unlike the ministers who distort its meaning. Stowe entitled one chapter about Eva (short for Evangeline) "The Little Evangelist." Eva's simple childlike faith makes her a model Christian for Stowe.

The idea that children are born innocent was a reversal of the notion that children inherit sin from Adam and Eve. By questioning this concept of original sin, liberal Protestants weakened the notion that Eve and all women bore more responsibility for sin and death than Adam. Now it was not human nature from which Christians needed to be saved but rather the immoral, male-dominated world.

None of the white men in Stowe's book live up to her standards as a true Christian. Instead she presents both women and African Americans as childlike and emotional and therefore as potential model Christians. Only Uncle Tom, of all the male characters, truly understands the Christian faith. The character of Uncle Tom has been criticized as a racist stereotype because he accepts his enslavement, reveres his white owners, and chooses to die rather than resist the brutal Simon Legree. For Stowe, enslaved African Americans resembled Christ because of their extraordinary suffering. As a group, they experienced over and over what she believed was the form of suffering most likely to draw souls to God, the loss of beloved children and parents. Women and slaves, in Stowe's novel, share experiences and qualities that incline them toward Christianity. They do not participate in the legislatures that pass laws defending the rights of slaveholders, do not join the teams of slave catchers who enforce those laws, and do not serve on the courts that uphold them. They do not own property and therefore do not participate in the economic sphere where slaves are traded and expedience wins over morality. Both women and slaves are excluded from power and therefore from the immoral influence of the public sphere. It is this view—that virtue derives from powerlessness—that has drawn criticism of Stowe's work in the twentieth century.

The home served as a religious haven also for the millions of immigrants who journeyed to the United States during the nineteenth and twentieth centuries. Coming from around the world, they quickly outnumbered the descendants of the British settlers. In the confines of the home, hallowed traditions could be observed even if they were ignored or condemned by the values of the new country. In the nineteenth century, the largest immigrant groups were Irish Catholics and Germans, who might be Catholic, Protestant, or Jewish. The turn of the century saw large influxes of Catholics from Italy and Poland, Protestants from Scandinavia, Jews from Russia and eastern Europe, and Orthodox Christians from Greece and eastern

Europe. Large twentieth-century immigrant groups include Chinese, Japanese, Koreans, and Filipinos, as well as diverse Latin American groups from Mexico, Central America, and the Caribbean. As each group joined the common culture of the United States, many saw the home as a place where they could maintain their own identities and hand them down to their children. The mother who ran the home often became the bearer of religious, as well as cultural, traditions.

Immigrant children usually attended public or Catholic schools, where they learned English, saluted the flag, and said the Pledge of Allegiance. But they came home after school to eat the foods of their parents' homelands and observe a variety of religious traditions. Most immigrants embraced the United States and were anxious to demonstrate their loyalty to their adopted country. But they were also loyal to the culture of their parents and grandparents. Because the United States required national loyalty but accepted religious pluralism, religion became the badge of ethnic identity for many immigrant groups.

The child from an observant Jewish family knew immediately that he or she had entered a Jewish space when arriving home from school. A *mezuzah* was nailed to the post of the entryway, whether a tenement apartment or a comfortable home. The *mezuzah* is a tiny box containing a parchment on which the most important prayer in Judaism, the *sh'ma*, is written in Hebrew. Adult men and women wore distinctive clothing required by religious law. Married women covered their hair with scarves or wigs to express modesty, and men wore special hats to remind them of the God above their heads. All food was prepared in accordance with *kashrut*, the Jewish dietary laws. Every meal was preceded by a *b'racha*, a prayer praising God for the food to be consumed.

Judaism is based on a covenant with God, in which Jews promise to obey the will of God, as represented by 613 positive and negative commandments that the rabbis have found in the Torah (Jewish scripture), and God promises to choose the Jewish people as his own from among the nations. Rabbinic law extends these commandments to govern every aspect of life, including how to conduct business, which side of the bed to get up on, when spouses should have sexual contact, what to eat, and what not to eat. The fulfillment of each law is called a *mitzvah* (plural *mitzvoth*). Women were excluded from positive *mitzvoth* that had to be performed at specified times because the rabbis assumed they had sole responsibility for raising children. Women could not read from the Torah during services. Instead, women were secluded behind a curtain or partition in the synagogue, so that they would not distract men from fulfilling their obligations to pray.

But many commandments could not be performed without women's cooperation. By keeping a kosher kitchen, a woman enabled her husband and children to fulfill Jewish law every time they put food in their mouths. Keeping kosher requires, among other things, a complete separation of milk and meat. This means not only that these items cannot be served at the same meal but that the same dishes or utensils cannot be used to prepare them. A pot used to cook meat can never be used to heat a baby's bottle. A knife used to slice cheese can never be used to cut meat. A spoon used to stir milk into coffee cannot be used to eat chicken soup. Once contaminated by touching the wrong type of food, a dish has to be purified according to a rabbi's recommendations, usually by being buried in the earth for several years or by being cleansed with fire. Some foods, such as pork or shellfish, are forbidden altogether. All food animals have to be killed in accordance with Jewish law by a *shohet*, a ritual slaughterer. No food can ever come in contact with anything that is not kosher.

Shopping as well as cooking was part of women's religious role. When observant Jewish women shop for food for their families, they buy it from Jewish merchants who understand Jewish law. Kosher meat must be purchased from a kosher butcher under rabbinic supervision. During the Passover holiday, an additional set of rules requires yet more dishes and special foods.

The most important Jewish holiday, the weekly observance of Shabbat (Sabbath), centers on the home. As with keeping kosher, the entire family depends on preparations made by the women of the house in observing Shabbat. Although women are excluded from many *mitzvoth*, four women's *mitzvoth* have been identified by the rabbis. Two of these involve Shabbat. On Friday nights, Jews are commanded to celebrate the Sabbath with a festive meal, but because all work is prohibited on Shabbat, preparations must be completed before sundown on Friday. When making challah, a special egg bread prepared for the occasion, a portion is set aside and burned in commemoration of the sacrifices made at the ancient temple in Jerusalem. This is the first "woman's *mitzvah*." The second is lighting candles to mark the beginning of Shabbat. Lighting Sabbath candles is accompanied by a prayer, as are all notable (and many ordinary) acts in Jewish life. The other women's *mitzvoth* are *mikvah*, the ritual bath used for purification after menstruation, and *niddah*, the laws governing the separation of the sexes during and following menstruation.

The relationship between cuisine and culture began with Jewish law, but it does not end there. Part of the function of keeping kosher is to keep Jews separate from other people. It prevents Jews from eating in the homes of non-Jews or in non-Jewish public settings. In the hostile anti-Semitic environments in which most Jews lived in Europe, Jews regarded such separation as necessary and beneficial. But as a growing number of modern Jews wanted to mix in American society, observance of *kashrut* was often limited to the home. This further emphasized the idea of the home as a religious sphere, in contrast with the non-Jewish public world.

By the third generation, however, only 10 percent of American-born Jews kept kosher. Most Jews abandoned the dietary restrictions to join the rest of the country in grating cheese onto spaghetti with meatballs and eating hamburgers with chocolate milkshakes. But traditional foods and the mothers who made them remained an important feature of American Judaism. In many homes, *kashrut* reappeared briefly on important holidays, and holiday foods took on great significance. A new genre of religious literature, the cookbook, emerged to assist with the preparation of Jewish foods using American ingredients. "Will we be wise enough to recognize the importance of these traditions and to hand them down intact to future generations?" asked a popular Jewish cookbook in 1945. "By the beautiful expedient of surrounding certain foods with the halo of religious associations…our mothers were able to preserve these traditions for us down through the ages," was its own reply.

Some holiday foods had explicit religious significance. Matzo, the unleavened bread eaten at Passover, commemorates the biblical story of the Jewish exodus from Egypt before the bread had time to rise. Latkes, the potato pancakes served on Hanukkah, are fried in oil because the holiday celebrates a miracle in which enough oil for one day kept the light in the ancient Jewish temple burning for eight days. Other foods, such as chicken soup, gefilte fish, and brisket, simply became associated with Jewish traditions because they were frequently served on Shabbat. Anything prepared in a kosher kitchen took on

Jewish associations. "If the dietary folkways are capable of striking a spiritual note in the home atmosphere, Jews cannot afford to disregard them," wrote Rabbi Mordecai Kaplan in *Judaism as a Civilization* (1934).

Favorite foods from the old country figured in many immigrant religious celebrations. Immigrant groups often centered their faith on home devotions learned from mothers and grandmothers rather than on official religious teachings. Like Harriet Beecher Stowe's fictional mothers, these mothers knew that religious teachings would take a firmer hold in their children if accompanied by special dishes that would remind them of national traditions. Indian mothers prepared special boxes of candy to exchange on Divali, the Hindu festival of lights. The aroma of sausage and peppers mingled at Italian saints' festivals, and Sikhs enjoyed a "sweet blessing" of specially prepared rice in their temples. The savory smells of such dishes indicated the arrival of important religious festivals. Among Catholics, many of these were devoted to the Madonna, the mother of Jesus. The Virgin's motherly role as a mediator who would intercede with her son on behalf of a faithful Catholic made her a natural symbol of cherished old-country ways.

Our Lady of Guadalupe, the patron saint of Mexico, plays this role for Mexican Americans. When the United States won California and much of the Southwest from Mexico in 1848, Mexican Catholics living in that territory became a part of the U.S. church structure. A long-running conflict began between American priests, who taught a Christ-centered faith at church and school, and Mexican-American women, who set up altars to Our Lady of Guadalupe in their homes and taught their children to pray to her.

According to tradition, devotion to Our Lady of Guadalupe began when the Virgin Mary appeared to Juan Diego, a Christian

Indian, on December 9, 1531, on a hill outside Mexico City. She told him that she wanted a church to be built on the site. Diego rushed to inform the Spanish bishop of the Virgin's request. The bishop assumed Diego had made up the story, but when Diego returned to the hill, he found roses blooming among the cactus and mesquite, although it was the middle of winter. Mary told him to take the roses to the bishop as proof of her appearance. When Diego unloaded the roses in the bishop's palace, an image of the Virgin appeared on the cloth in which he had wrapped them. That image is displayed today in the huge church built on that site, where millions of pilgrims travel to see it every year.

The image of Our Lady of Guadalupe combined Indian symbolism with that of Catholicism. Most important, Mary herself had the features of an Indian woman as well as those of the Spanish conquerors who brought Catholicism to Mexico. She offered comfort to a suffering people struggling under the domination of the Spanish. "I am thy merciful mother...I shall listen to all your sorrows and free you from all your misery, grief and anguish," the Virgin promised her faithful. As Mexico developed into a mestizo (racially mixed) country, in which Indian and Spanish traditions blended into a new culture, Our Lady of Guadalupe became the focus of devotion and pride for Mexican Catholics. She became a national as well as a religious symbol. While showing faithfulness to the mother of Jesus, her devotees also affirmed their Mexican origins and traditions. As millions of Mexicans joined the ranks of U.S. Catholicism, Our Lady of Guadalupe grew in importance in the United States.

An image of Our Lady of Guadalupe often occupies the central position in a home altar that includes photographs of living and dead family members as well as statues or pictures of other saints. The Virgin is literally part of the home circle. Women turn to her with intimate problems and domestic troubles, just as they might turn to their own mother. "She brings me comfort," said a Mexican-American mother in California in the 1990s. "Ever since I had my children, I feel she knows what I mean. She knows how I feel and I can talk to her woman to woman, mother to mother." When family members are unconcerned or unavailable, Guadalupe is always there, never abandoning her faithful. Because the Virgin suffered as a mother who lost her precious son, she understands the grief of human mothers trying to raise children in difficult circumstances.

For many Mexican-American Catholics, the regular rituals of the church pale in significance when compared to religious ceremonies marking important family events. Baptisms, First Communions, weddings, and funerals draw large crowds to churches that may be nearly empty on most Sundays. The Virgin's feast day is among the most important celebrations because it focuses attention on the central figure within the family, the mother. Statues of the Virgin are taken out of the church to be paraded through the streets as Our Lady of Guadalupe visits her people. She also serves as a role model for Mexican-American women. "Our Lady of Guadalupe represents to me everything we as a people should strive to be," another woman said, "strong yet humble, warm and compassionate, yet courageous enough to stand up for what we believe in." As women pray to the Virgin, they also try to imagine what she would do in their shoes. The image of Our Lady of Guadalupe combines in one figure the ideal Catholic, the ideal woman and mother, and the ideal Mexican.

Other Catholic groups that brought devotions with them to the United States focused on appearances of the Virgin in other times and places. Italians brought Our Lady of Mount Carmel to East Harlem in New York City. There a Virgin with distinctly Italian features listened to the woes of Italian immigrant mothers. Polish and Hungarian immigrants brought their Virgins as well. Like Mexicans, all these groups believed that being a good Catholic, being a good woman, and following national traditions were inseparable.

American daughters, however, often chafed at the restrictions of old-country ways. Anzia Yezierska, a Jewish immigrant writer, subtitled her 1925 autobiographical novel *Bread Givers* "a conflict between a father of the old world and a daughter of the new." In it she recounted how her old-world father expected his daughters to marry young men of his choosing and to devote themselves to endless housework. Instead, Yezierska's heroine hoped to "make herself for a person" by pursuing an education, becoming a teacher, and marrying for love. After a bitter struggle for independence from her family and the immigrant community, she found she could not really be herself if she abandoned them completely. At the end of the book, she and the husband she has chosen herself decide to keep a kosher home so that her aged father can live out his days with them. Like many American daughters, she found herself faced with difficult choices between cherished traditions and new opportunities.

Such conflicts could be especially difficult for Asian-American women. They brought with them religious ideas about the restriction of women's activities to the home that were even more rigid than those they found in America. Confucian philosophy had shaped social relations in China, Japan, and Korea since the fifth century BCE. Like Puritanism, Confucianism held that social harmony depended on the subjugation of inferiors to superiors. It also viewed the family as the basic social unit through which such values should be enacted. Instead of viewing women as inferior to their husbands but superior to their children or servants, however, Confucianism placed all men above all women. "Obedience to father; obedience to husband;

obedience to son" were the cardinal principles for women's behavior. Female babies were considered undesirable because women joined their husband's family at marriage and had no continuing obligations to their own parents or relatives. Because the family was defined as a continuing male line, women were excluded from ancestor worship. They managed all relevant preparations, cooked the proper foods, and set up the ritual table, but they did not join in the ceremonies.

The first Asians to come to the United States were Chinese men who worked on the railroads in the West in the mid-nineteenth century. They were prohibited by law from bringing female family members with them, and Chinese were virtually excluded from entrance by federal laws of 1882, 1892, 1902, and 1904. The restriction against women left a 95 percent male Chinese community and encouraged the smuggling of young women to work as indentured prostitutes. Because Chinese workers were the first to be excluded, the few women who entered the country legally were the wives of merchants. These women often had the bound feet that marked women of privileged classes in China. From a young age, their feet were wrapped in bandages until the toes were permanently bent under and the whole foot compressed to a few inches in length. Considered a sign of gentility and beauty, bound feet confined women to the home because they were physically incapable of walking beyond it. Some Asian countries also had laws prohibiting women from walking in public. The idea that modern China needed women's contributions and the influence of Protestant missionaries led to the outlawing of foot-binding in China in 1911. But the belief that a woman's destiny was to serve her husband's family persisted both in China and the United States.

Legal discrimination and cultural prohibitions discouraged many Asian women from moving to the United States.

Most Asian-American populations did not achieve a balance between men and women until the 1960s. Asian-American Protestant churches were important in helping women who had succeeded in entering the country adjust to their new home, whether they were already Christians or converted upon arrival. This was especially true for Koreans who entered the United States in large numbers after the Immigration Reform Act of 1965 lifted quotas that had placed severe limits on their entrance. Protestant churches composed exclusively of Korean Americans became the center of the ethnic community. In the 1990s only 20 percent of the people are church members in Korea, but 80 percent of Korean immigrants in the United States belong to a church. Women constitute 70 percent of church members in both Korea and the United States.

Kim Ai Ra grew up in Korea, in a family that believed daughters should be as well educated as sons. After graduating from college, she came to the United States in 1962 for an arranged marriage to a man she had never met. She found that both the Korean community and the larger society in which she now lived viewed her as a nobody whose identity derived exclusively from her husband's. She tried to belittle herself in order to fit into the role that was expected of her. "Here, the Korean immigrant churches became my saviors...legitimating my self-denunciation," she wrote with irony. Now biblical texts justified Confucian principles requiring women's subjection to men. After twenty-five years of marriage, she rebelled, attending graduate school and conducting a study of women in Korean churches. She found that these churches encouraged traditions requiring women to sacrifice themselves for their families. The churches followed Korean customs that excluded women from all leadership roles, even in denominations (Presbyterian or Methodist) that followed different practices in the United States. The main role in church affairs assigned to women's organizations was cooking Korean meals.

The high rate of church membership in the Korean-American community and the high rate of women's participation suggest that women derived substantial benefits from their churches even if their roles were limited within them. Churches offered an alternative in a society that stigmatized Asian women as passive servants or as sexual exotics. In addition, the churches provided a safe and familiar community in an alien land, a place where the Korean language could be spoken and preserved, a place where potential marriage partners could meet.

Like women in all conservative churches, Korean-American women faced a dilemma as a result of the relatively low numbers of male members in their churches. Christian doctrine warned against being "yoked to an unbeliever." But men constituted only 30 percent of church members, and marriage and mother-hood remained women's most important religious roles. Women inevitably married men who did not share their beliefs. How could Christian women be obedient to husbands who were not themselves Christian? Religious women engaged in a constant struggle to abide by the contradictory tenets of their faith. The idea that women should sacrifice themselves for their families encouraged them to accept such situations.

Although religious ideals emphasizing women's respon-sibilities for home and family limited opportunities for self-fulfillment, they also provided compelling benefits. Whatever their religion or their country of origin, women found sustenance in their faith, which helped them hold families together in difficult circumstances. The necessary work of child rearing and house-hold labor might otherwise seem like drudgery. But as part of one's religious destiny, it assumed meaning and value. While the public world of politics and economics might ignore or denigrate the roles to which women dedicated their lives, religious institutions affirmed and valued them. Denied the possibility of respect for any activities outside the home, mothers could identify with the divine women of sacred history who won reverence through self-sacrifice.

The Cherokees are an important tribal group who lived in southeast-ern North America at the time of British settlement. In the early 1800s, the Cherokees were forcibly removed from their homelands to make way for American settlement. Women had a say in the domestic policies of the tribe, as well as in matters of war and peace, occasion-ally joining their husbands and brothers on the battlefield. Cherokee women who were particularly honored and influential were given the title "Beloved Woman." As the last Beloved Woman of the Chero-kee nation, Nancy (Nanyehi) Ward served as head of the Cherokee women's council, which gave her great influence as well as a vote on the council of head chiefs and warriors. This 1817 letter from Nancy Ward is addressed to the chief's council. In it she expresses Cherokee women's opposition to the sale of tribal lands in Georgia.

The Cherokee ladys now being present at the meeting of the Chiefs and warriors in council have thought it their duties as mothers to address their beloved Chiefs and warriors now assembled.

Our beloved children and head men of the Cherokee nation we address you warriors in council we have raised all of you on the land which we now have, which God gave us to inhabit and raise provisions we know that our country has once been exten-sive but by repeated sales has become circumscribed to a small tract and never thought it our duty to interfere in the disposi-tion of it till now, if a father or mother was to sell all their lands which they had to depend on which their children had to raise their living on which would be indeed bad and to be removed to another country we do not wish to go to an unknown country which we have understood some of our children wish to go over the Mississippi but this act of our children would be like destroying your mothers. You mothers your sisters ask and beg of you not to part with any more of our lands, we say ours you are descendants and take pity on our request, but keep it for our growing children for it was the good will of our creator to place here and you know our father the great president will not allow his white children to take our country away only keep your hands off of paper talks for it is our own country for if it was not they would not ask you to put your hands to paper for it would be impossible to remove us all for as soon as one child is raised we have others in our arms for such is our situation and will consider our circumstance. Therefore children don't part with any more of our lands but continue on it and enlarge your farms and cultivate and raise corn and cotton and we your mothers and sisters will make clothing for you which our father the president has recommended to us all we don't charge anybody for selling our lands, but we have heard such intentions of our children but your talks become true at last and it was our desire to forewarn you all not to part with our lands.

Nancy Ward to her children Warriors to take pity and listen to the talks of your sisters, although I am very old yet cannot but pity the situation in which you will hear of their minds. I have great many grand children which I wish they to do well on our land.

CHAPTER 4

Organized Womanhood

In the fall of 1873, the women of Hillsborough, Ohio, decided it was time to take action against the abuse of alcohol in their community. After a temperance meeting in a local church, they marched in a group to one of the town's thirteen saloons. They entered the saloon, knelt on the floor, and began to pray and sing hymns. When the owner asked them to leave, they refused to do so as long as he continued to sell liquor. Few male patrons wanted to drink in the presence of so many praying women. Eventually the tavern keeper agreed to end liquor sales. Strengthened by their success, the women met at church again the next day and marched to another saloon. Within a few weeks, nine of the thirteen businesses selling alcohol in Hillsborough had closed and the women in nearby towns had taken up the campaign to close saloons in their communities.

The Ohio Women's Crusade gave rise to the first nondenominational national organization of Protestant women: the Woman's Christian Temperance Union (WCTU), founded in 1874. After the Civil War, women across the country joined in national organizations like the WCTU that helped shape U.S. politics and religion, as well as the women themselves. Secular women's organizations, including those devoted to women's rights, flowered after the war, but religiously motivated activities drew much larger numbers of women. As new immigrant groups arrived in the United States, they followed the model set by groups such as the WCTU. In the twentieth century, American women organized the largest Jewish organization in the world, Hadassah, the Women's Zionist Organization of America. Such national organizations of religious women played an important role in shaping public life.

Religious concerns prompted the formation of the first formal women's organizations in the United States. In fact, before 1820 local churches were virtually the only places American women came together outside the home to organize groups and pursue common goals. Discouraged from speaking in front of men, women gathered in prayer meetings where they could freely discuss God's working in their lives. Later, these prayer meetings started to take on special functions. "Mothers' meetings" convened to pray for the conversion of members' children. Missionary societies pooled their resources and raised money for the education of ministers, for the support of their own churches, and for the founding of new ones. Clergymen encouraged these efforts, and the idea that women's pious influence could and should affect other people's behavior increasingly gained acceptance. The church was the only public space where women's presence was accepted and appreciated, and it became the point of departure for women's entrance into public life.

Energized by the evangelical enthusiasm of the nineteenth century, Protestant women organized to change society in a variety of ways. In part as a response to the proliferation of Protestant associations blending social services with the promotion of evangelical values, Jewish and Catholic women also united to build orphanages and hospitals, to run Sunday schools, and to encourage temperance and chastity. For women, belonging to an organization where one might be asked to hold an elective office or approach male civic leaders about the group's concerns marked a watershed in the expansion of roles outside the home.

Even before Protestant women banded together to fight social ills, Roman Catholic nuns, also called sisters, united for the purpose of changing society. Beginning with a convent and school for girls in New Orleans in 1727, organizations of nuns established themselves throughout the country. Committing their lives exclusively to their religious faith, nuns take vows of chastity, poverty, and obedience in an effort to replace earthly desires with divine goals. There are few parallel roles for women among Protestants, Jews, or Muslims. Nuns are full-time religious professionals who represent the Catholic Church and promote its teachings. But they are subject to the religious authority of ordained priests.

Before the 1960s sisters lived in communities composed exclusively of women and ran institutions staffed exclusively by women. In these separate settings women enjoyed great authority and autonomy—probably more than the vast majority of their female contemporaries. But their vow of obedience meant that the entire order must obey the direction of the all-male hierarchy of priests and bishops and, finally, of the pope.

Beyond vows of chastity, poverty, and obedience, each order of nuns had its own rule, dictating specific devotional practices, dress, and goals. The long flowing habit of each order, with its distinctive head covering, concealed differences among individual women, melding them into a community united toward a common purpose. The names of orders reflected the focus of their devotions or the source of their rule: Ursulines took their name from the virgin martyr princess St. Ursula while Benedictines followed the monastic rule written by St. Benedict in the sixth century. Training focused on the spiritual rewards of humility, selflessness, and religious discipline. Upon taking her vows, each sister had her hair cut off, donned the habit, and received a new name to signal her departure from "the world" and her new identity as part of a community of women committed to God's work.

One such woman was Mother Mary Caroline, the first American superior of the Poor School Sisters of Notre Dame. Born Josephine Friess in Bavaria, she received her new name when she entered a German convent at age eighteen. As a novice, she learned the order's ways and prepared to become a full member of the religious community. After taking her final vows, she was one of four sisters who traveled to the United States as missionaries to the large population of German immigrants. She became the head of the order's American branch in 1850, when she established a convent in Milwaukee.

Working without pay and often with few resources, sisters devoted themselves to providing the services that sustained Catholic life in the United States. In the single year of 1858, for example, the School Sisters of Notre Dame founded an orphanage in New Orleans housing 120 poor children, a second orphanage in Baltimore housing seventy-five, and two schools in Wisconsin, one in Watertown and one in Kenosha. Each mission required the establishment of a convent for sisters and facilities for the children they served.

More than two hundred women's orders were operating in the United States by 1911, each a testament to the astounding accomplishments of Catholic nuns. In 1900 sisters operated 3,811 parochial (church-run) schools, 663 academies for girls (and 102 for boys), and 265 hospitals. The Sisters of Mercy are among the largest providers of health care in the United States. In addition to their major work of teaching and nursing, nuns ran child-care facilities, orphanages, mental institutions, settlement houses, residences for working women and for unwed mothers, and homes for delinquent girls. Nuns oversaw an empire of interlocking institutions that constituted Catholic social services in most U.S. cities and towns, providing the foundation of their church's distinctive culture.

The mass migration of Catholics into the United States in the nineteenth century was accompanied by a dramatic increase in the anti-Catholic sentiment that had always lurked in American Protestantism and popular culture. Because Protestants rejected the Catholic belief that celibacy is an aid to piety and because they considered the family the central Christian institution, they targeted their hostility at nuns. Nuns felt forced to wear secular clothing when they traveled away from their convents to avoid any unfriendly attention. The idea of a community of unmarried women supervised by unmarried men (priests) fueled weird fantasies in the minds of non-Catholics. Lurid tales of immorality behind convent walls, narrated by purported escaped nuns, became popular. After an especially virulent anti-Catholic sermon by Lyman Beecher, a mob attacked and burned the Ursuline convent in Boston in 1834.

In this hostile environment, the establishment of Catholic social services became a religious as well as a social priority. The millions of Catholics who made their faith the nation's largest by 1860 were for the most part impoverished immigrants exiled by hunger from countries where Catholics were in the majority. When a million Irish Catholics immigrated to the United States to avoid illness and starvation in the potato famine of the 1840s, European orders sent sisters to help them maintain a Catholic identity in a Protestant country. The only charities serving the needy in the United States were Protestant, and they treated Catholicism as a moral failing that had caused such poverty. Public education included Bible reading from a distinctly Protestant perspective. Catholics needed their own schools, hospitals, orphanages, and asylums if they were to survive as a distinct faith in the United States. In 1884 Catholic bishops recognized the need for the type of separate institutions operated by nuns. The Third Plenary Council of American Bishops passed a resolution making the establishment of a Catholic school the highest priority of every parish, even before building a church. It was the unpaid labor of nuns as teachers that made the fulfillment of this goal possible.

Until 1809, all Catholic orders in the United States were branches of European orders. In that year, however, Elizabeth Seton founded the Sisters of Charity in Emmitsburg, Maryland. Seton had converted to Catholicism after the death of her husband in 1803. Before his death she had been a loyal Episcopalian who enjoyed the theater, balls, and the charitable work of New York society. As a widow with no means of support, Seton was ostracized by her family because she adopted the Catholic faith. She struggled to support her five children by running a boardinghouse. In 1808 she accepted an invitation to start a school for Catholic girls in Baltimore, a city with a sizable Catholic elite, who later sent their daughters to the new school. Seton took her first vows before Baltimore's Archbishop John Carroll in 1809. Mother Seton's unusual piety and sincere devotion to her "spiritual daughters" drew many members to her order, which quickly spread beyond Maryland to Philadelphia and New York. Canonized in 1975, Elizabeth Seton was the first North American to receive this official recognition from the Catholic Church.

Bishops and parish priests valued the presence of women's orders because they needed the services that sisters offered. At the same time, they sought to control sisters' activities and ensure that the orders submitted to clerical authority. Women's orders had less freedom than men's monastic orders because, like all women in American society, nuns were assumed to need the guidance of men and were prohibited by law from conducting their own financial and legal affairs. Just as other women were assumed to derive their identities primarily from their relationship to men as wives and mothers, nuns were considered "brides of Christ" and were subject to the authority of ecclesiastical superiors, who could overturn decisions made by a mother superior and could even remove or replace the superiors who led women's orders. For the most part, religious women not only agreed to be subservient to male clerics but embraced the role. Women who chose to enter monastic orders, after all, were both products and promoters of a culture and a church that stressed women's subservience as a religious virtue. Sisters, like many of their Protestant counterparts, taught that "glorious submissiveness" was a woman's highest calling, whether she submitted to husband, priest, religious superior, or God.

But the actual work that nuns undertook in the United States belied the notion that they would do whatever they were told. To fulfill the pressing needs of the American Catholic community, most orders abandoned or modified the rule of enclosure that confined religious women in Europe to their convents and strictly limited their contact with the secular world. The many social services nuns performed in the United States required not only frequent contact with those outside their orders but even interaction with non-Catholics.

The role of religious sisters has been especially important because there are so many more nuns than priests. In 1820 there were 270 sisters in the United States, and 150 priests. By 1900, however, forty thousand nuns outnumbered priests by four to one. The number of nuns reached its peak in 1966, when more than 180,000 American women served in Catholic orders. As women's opportunities for professional training, service, and intellectual development outside the church expanded in the 1960s and 1970s, the number professing a religious vocation declined dramatically.

The lives of nuns embodied the contradictions between the active roles they assumed in building U.S. Catholicism and the passive roles they aspired to as servants of God. "To foster and preserve the spirit of our congregation, the voluntary renunciation of one's own will, in a land where the spirit of independence prevails in every phase of life, is indeed difficult," wrote Mother Mary Caroline. She complained that American girls took longer to be trained as nuns than those in her native Bavaria because "in early childhood they were not trained to obedience, submission, and self-denial." They needed these qualities, she believed, to devote themselves fully to the salvation of the children entrusted to their care. But at the same time, she believed such "holy and strenuous work" required "manlike firmness and indomitable patience and prudence." This was the double legacy of nuns to American Catholic women: They taught subservience and passivity while they practiced stoic strength and independent action. They preached obedience to men but they chose to live in communities of women.

Protestant women who wanted to devote their lives to service lacked the structure provided by Catholic women's orders. Instead they started volunteer organizations such as the Woman's Christian Temperance Union to pursue their goals for the transformation of society. Many Americans saw temperance as a women's issue because its advocates depicted men's drinking as the source of poverty and violence for the women who were legally and economically dependent on them. Women's rights advocate Susan B. Anthony, for example, started off as a temperance speaker.

One of the most popular novels of the nineteenth century, Timothy Shay Arthur's *Ten Nights in a Bar Room* (1854), told the story of little Mary Morgan, who died from an injury received when she went to a saloon to retrieve her drunken father. On her deathbed she extracted a promise from her father not to return to the saloon until after she was better, a time that would never come. This story presents two long-lived attitudes about liquor consumption in the United States: that women and girls were the victims of men's alcohol abuse but also the solution to it. Through faith and love, a Christian woman could save a man from drink, but, like Jesus, she must be willing to sacrifice her life in the process. Calling itself "organized mother-love," the WCTU built its arguments on the first half of this assumption without conceding to the second.

Excessive alcohol consumption was a real problem in the nineteenth-century United States. Liquor sales fell before the Civil War, due in part to the success of the temperance movement, but increased during and after the war. The number of saloons rose dramatically, reaching one for every two hundred people in many places by the 1870s. Wives and children of alcoholics were extraordinarily vulnerable because, in most states, women possessed no rights to the custody of their children, and all their property, including current wages, belonged to their husbands.

The women's temperance movement was far more than a campaign to help individual women victimized by alcoholic men. Temperance work became the primary way American women increased their involvement in public life. By the 1880s the

WCTU was the largest organization of women the United States had ever known, with chapters in every state and major city and thousands of local communities. By the end of the century there were unions in twenty countries beyond the United States, many of them continuing to provide an important political voice for women long after the American union began to decline in the twentieth century.

The period of the WCTU's greatest political influence coincided with the presidency of Frances Willard, who served from 1879 until her death in 1898. It was said that she "could move fifty thousand women as she moved her right arm." Under her direction, the WCTU became a powerful organization dedicated to reforming society according to the values of Protestant women. Willard's famous "do everything policy" aptly described the breadth of WCTU interests and campaigns. By the end of her presidency, twenty-five of the organization's fifty-nine departments dealt with issues other than temperance. These included the reform of prisons, the establishment of day nurseries, kindergartens, medical clinics, industrial schools, and homes for unwed mothers and destitute women, as well as the care of orphans, abused children, and prostitutes. Other developments addressed labor issues, evangelism, tobacco use, peace and arbitration, and the promotion of Sabbath observance, to name a few.

The vote for women was one of the first nontemperance issues to attract the WCTU's attention. During the last quarter of the nineteenth century the WCTU became the largest organization promoting woman suffrage, far larger than the groups devoted exclusively to that purpose. Willard advocated woman suffrage because she believed that only with the vote could women bring about the prohibition of alcoholic beverages. She coined the motto "The Ballot for Home Protection" to indicate that voting did not conflict with the idea of woman as the guardian of the home but simply extended her role into the public sphere.

However it was phrased, the idea that women needed the vote in order to promote Christian values was a radical notion to the relatively conservative churchwomen who made up the rank and file of the WCTU. Leaders faced an enormous challenge in convincing members to seek a larger role in public affairs, including the vote. Most WCTU members were women whose families were prosperous enough to spare some of their labor. Often freed from household work by Irish or German maids (in the North) or by African Americans (in the South), members thought of themselves as respectable ladies who shunned public roles and whose economic privilege allowed them to confine their activities to home and church.

The vote symbolized all the departures from the private sphere required by the WCTU's "do everything policy." Members needed to be convinced not only that God did not object to their leaving their homes to vote but that he wanted them to seek the vote. Willard herself described her adoption of the suffrage cause as a Christian conversion experience. Alone in her room, praying on her knees following a Sunday morning Bible study, she received a message that she was "to speak for women's ballots as a weapon of protection to her home." Willard firmly believed that God placed this impression in her mind, and many other WCTU leaders reported similar conversions.

As active churchwomen, WCTU members had all heard religious arguments for the restriction of women's activities to the home. Ministers argued that the moral influence of women, upon which the progress of Christianity depended, would be undermined if women stepped out of the home and entered the public sphere. In *Woman Suffrage: The Reform against Nature*

(1869), the popular Congregationalist minister Horace Bushnell argued that men were created to govern, and women to be governed, and that women would unsex themselves in the act of voting.

Willard and other WCTU leaders, however, saw women's public activism as an extension of the familiar roles as protectors of purity and piety. Voting, they believed, would advance these goals, not conflict with them. Women, with their pastors' encouragement, already took responsibility for the moral, physical, and spiritual welfare of fathers, sons, and brothers. Now, WCTU leaders argued, they should extend their motherly concerns to all of society. "Mother-hearted women are called to be the saviors of the race," Willard told the women of the United States. Just as God's all-embracing love saved humanity from sin through the sacrifice of his son, women who expressed a mother's sacrificial love in the public realm could save society. By voting for the prohibition of alcohol and for a host of other social reforms, women, like Christ, could lift humanity out of sin.

By making public action compatible with domestic values, the Woman's Christian Temperance Union significantly expanded the political role of American women but also limited its effect. The evangelical outlook that served as a basis for the WCTU's program united women from North and South and from city and farm, making it the first truly national women's organization. But the Protestant values that united many women excluded others. Like other white Protestant reformers of their day, WCTU members feared immigration from Catholic countries and believed that Catholic immigrants did not value U.S. democracy or the system of public education that trained citizens to participate in it. Union members hoped to redeem America in specifically evangelical terms, by giving the force of law to the Sunday Sabbath, by demanding the use of the Bible in public schools, and by calling for the prohibition of alcohol. These goals conflicted with the rights of other Americans and would eventually make the WCTU appear too narrow to represent all American women. Nevertheless, later organizations would succeed in getting the federal government to adopt many programs inspired by the WCTU's emphasis on maternal values as the basis for reform. These included programs to supply maternal and infant health care and to provide aid to families with dependent children. The emergence of a wide range of government-sponsored welfare programs in the twentieth century perhaps owes more to the social vision of Protestant women as expressed in the WCTU than to the secular women's rights movement that ultimately succeeded in winning the vote.

Even before the temperance cause captured their imagination, Protestant women worked together in the missionary movement, which eventually outstripped the temperance movement in gaining their loyalty. Emboldened by phenomenal growth in their churches and the increasing influence of Evangelicalism in public life, American Protestants began a mass movement to spread their faith around the world. Much of the dramatic growth of this movement resulted from the rise of women's missionary societies. Between 1861 and 1894, women's foreign missionary societies were founded in thirty-three denominations, and home missionary societies in seventeen. These included black and white churches as well as most immigrant denominations such as Dutch Reform or Swedish Lutheran. The combined membership of women's missionary societies reached approximately three million at its height in the 1920s, outpacing women's involvement in any other cause or organization.

Stories of the mission field have long inspired the piety of American women. Memoirs of the physical, emotional, and spiritual hardships of raising children in distant lands remained popular throughout the nineteenth and much of the twentieth century. The difficult lives and premature deaths of early missionary wives made them models of the self-denial to which all Christian women aspired. Harriet Newell, who died in childbirth in India in 1812, won special admiration. "Should I refuse to make this sacrifice, refuse to lend my little aid in promulgation of the gospel amongst the heathen, how could I ever expect to enjoy the blessing of God, and peace of conscience, though surrounded with every temporal mercy?" she asked. The willingness of women missionaries to give up the comforts of home and family inspired those who remained behind.

Women like Harriet Newell were expected to educate and evangelize the women and children of the mission station as well as care for their missionary husbands, bear and rear children, and conduct a Christian household as a model for converted Christians. When these expectations proved unrealistic, male missionaries concluded that the most important role for a missionary wife was to establish a Christian home. American women endorsed this goal, but they also believed the considerable talents of women missionaries deserved a broader scope. They began to organize separate societies devoted to sending single women into missionary service who would dedicate themselves explicitly to the needs of women and children.

American women adopted the mission cause with unprecedented zeal. Missionary society members raised huge amounts of money and practiced management skills on a large scale, both in overseas enterprises and in their massive national organizations. Women throughout the United States educated themselves about the countries where they sponsored missions, studied geography and history, and listened anxiously to the reports of returned missionaries. On the northern prairies, Norwegian Lutheran farm wives traveled long distances by horse-drawn cart to gather for one day each month to quilt and read aloud the latest mission publication about their church's activities in Madagascar or New Guinea. Missions to Africa were of special concern to the women of black denominations. Middle-class women with leisure time welcomed the intellectual stimulation of mission meetings, often becoming serious students of the cultures in which they supported missions.

These new organizations were motivated by the idea that women throughout the world shared a common nature and common needs. *Women's Work for Women*, the title of the Presbyterian monthly magazine, became the movement's motto. United to the women of the world by maternal self-sacrifice, American Protestants believed they had a special duty to improve the conditions of motherhood in foreign lands and felt a spiritual bond with the women they hoped to convert. In most parts of Asia, local customs denied male missionaries access to women. Only female missionaries could enter the quarters of upper-class women in India, China, or Turkey. American women were horrified by stories of foot-binding in China and of young widows thrown on their husbands' funeral pyres in India. Firmly convinced that other religions degraded women, whereas Christianity elevated them, American women threw themselves into missionary work, the enterprise they believed could do more than any other to improve women's lot around the world.

The idea of women's work for women shifted the focus of missionary programs. Whereas male missionaries focused mainly on evangelism, women's organizations sponsored a host of social services intended to improve the lot of women in other countries. Women's groups built schools, hospitals, and orphanages, greatly increasing the credibility of the missionary enterprise among those they hoped to help. In the mission field women could preach, teach, run schools and hospitals, and criticize customs harmful to women, but when they returned home they were barred from the pulpits of most churches. Instead, they thrilled audiences composed exclusively of their own sex, inspiring them to ever greater support for missions. By 1909 women's societies supported close to five thousand unmarried women missionaries, twice the number of the male missionaries sent by the general societies.

Both the idea of women's work for women and the experiences of women missionaries caused conflict with male church leaders. This was especially true for home missionaries, who worked among poor or non-Protestant populations in the United States. In San Francisco, for example, Presbyterian women met bitter opposition when they founded a rescue home for Chinese prostitutes. Like the men of their church, they saw Chinese immigration as a threat to U.S. institutions. But unlike the men, they opposed the Chinese Exclusion Act of 1882, which prohibited the entrance of Chinese laborers. They believed that putting Protestant morality to work by rescuing these women was a more effective solution than legal exclusion.

Common interests among women sometimes helped overcome the racial barriers that divided U.S. society. Because discriminatory laws passed at the turn of the century excluded blacks from most public accommodations, the women of the National Baptist Convention U.S.A., Inc.—the country's largest organization of African Americans—focused on home missions to address the pressing needs of their communities. They formed an unexpected alliance with the women's home missionary society of the American Baptist Convention, composed of white northerners, which provided financial assistance for the founding of several educational enterprises. These included Spelman College in Atlanta, the first black women's college. Although the white Baptist women hoped that women's education would inspire decorum in black neighborhoods and squash tendencies toward rebellion, African-American women viewed women's education as a necessity for promoting the goals of their own communities. Though motivated by different goals, black and white Baptists could agree on a single program based on the centrality of women's moral role.

Women missionaries left a complicated legacy in the countries and communities where they served. Another magazine title, *Heathen Woman's Friend*, published by the Methodists, expressed the irony of the claim that all women are the same. It included condescending assumptions about the inferiority of non-Protestant cultures. The self-righteous claims of American women make many of their efforts easy for us to dismiss as unconscious extensions of American imperialism. However, the success of women's missionary enterprises suggests that, on the whole, they were indeed appealing to those they hoped to help. In many places Americans founded the first secondary schools, colleges, and graduate schools for women. Still, women experienced conflicts as they took advantage of the new opportunities. For a Korean woman who sought an education, for example, the advantages of Christianity were obvious but the price was high. Conversion meant she could pursue her education but could also mean alienation from her family, unless they, too, converted. Stories abound of loyal Buddhist and Hindu women hungry for education who entered mission schools because there was no alternative and ultimately adopted Christianity. Ironically, the fact that opportunities for women's education were often tied to Christianization has contributed to a backlash today. Contemporary nationalist movements (especially in Muslim countries) sometimes restrict opportunities for women when those movements question the value of Western culture in favor of the revival of their own religion and traditions.

The legacy of missionary societies in the United States is more straightforward. While the temperance movement thrust women into unprecedented leadership roles in local and occasionally state government and public institutions, the women's missionary movement transformed women's roles within the churches. In most Protestant denominations the women's missionary society was the only national body representing the women of the church. Women who were not allowed to vote in local churches or in other religious organizations elected their own officers from among their members. If church leaders wanted to communicate with female members, they had to turn to the missionary society. The respect accorded these leaders was so great that Helen Barrett Montgomery, who headed the American Baptist Woman's Foreign Missionary Society as well as interdenominational efforts, was elected president of the American Baptist Convention in 1920, becoming the first woman ever to hold that post. Even after women gained the right to vote in political elections in 1919, they still could not vote or hold church office in many Protestant denominations. The mammoth accomplishments of women's mission societies, however, in fund-raising, organization, and education made church leaders question the legitimacy of women's exclusion from lay rights within the churches.

In the 1920s and 1930s the very success of the women's missionary societies led to their undoing. Male church leaders wanted more control over the women's money and programs. They argued that women's organizations should be combined with the general missionary societies presided over by men. The era of separate spheres had come to an end, and a new generation of young women agreed that they would rather participate as equals in mixed societies. But the price of equality was high. Women lost their autonomy and their separate voice in the church when they lost their separate organizations. In most churches they won lay rights, but they lost the separate empire devoted to women's concerns over which they had presided for half a century.

While Protestant women organized to provide health care for women around the world, American Jewish women organized to provide an alternative system so that Jewish babies in Palestine would not have to be born in Christian hospitals, where they would be baptized. Hadassah, the Women's Zionist Organization of America, was founded in 1912 by Henrietta Szold to provide health care for the residents of Palestine. Zionism was an international movement to establish a Jewish state in Palestine. Hadassah was America's first national Zionist organization, and it has remained the largest. For much of its history, in fact, Hadassah has been the largest Jewish organization in the world.

Henrietta Szold founded Hadassah after a twenty-year career as a writer and translator ended in frustration. Distraught over the lack of recognition and acceptance available to a woman in the world of Jewish scholarship, Szold and her mother embarked from New York City on a trip to Palestine in 1910. Shocked by the poverty and lack of medical care and sanitation she witnessed there, Szold decided to found an organization of women devoted to practical medical work in Palestine. In doing so she hoped to alleviate both the dire conditions in Palestine and the problems facing Jewish women in America. "There is no more serious charge made against Judaism," Szold wrote in 1915, "than the charge that women are neglected." Excluded from Jewish education and synagogue worship, American women lacked an official way to express their Jewish identity. Hadassah provided just the vehicle they needed, and it became the first organization to reflect the central role that Zionism would play in American Jewish identity.

Zionism was not a popular cause in the United States before World War II. A small, impoverished Jewish community had remained in Palestine since the main body of Jews was expelled in the first century. Through centuries of exile in Europe and Asia, Jews maintained a religious belief that God would one day return them to the land he gave them, the land of Israel. As minorities in the countries where they lived in Europe, Jews possessed no political rights. With the rise of anti-Semitism in the ninteenth and twentieth centuries, the religious hope of return to Israel became a political imperative for Jews. Zionists argued that the only way Jews could survive escalating persecution was to establish their own state, from which they could never be expelled.

Zionism had a clear appeal in Europe, where many governments were openly anti-Semitic. But in the United States, Jews who had fled repressive conditions in Europe felt they had found a permanent home. Most wanted to emphasize their connection to the United States rather than to Israel. Hadassah was in the vanguard of a dramatic reversal in which Zionism became a hallmark of American Jewish identity.

Founded at the height of the women's missionary movement, Hadassah was similar to its Protestant counterparts. Its success lay in its tireless focus on areas considered to be appropriate for women: health and education. Within a year two visiting nurses established the first Hadassah clinic in Palestine to treat Jewish children for trachoma, a common eye disease. Over the decades this grew into a network of hospitals, nurses' training schools, nutrition programs, infant and maternal welfare centers, and educational programs that would form the foundation of public social services when Israel became an independent state in 1948. With the rise of Nazism in Germany in the 1930s, Hadassah helped sponsor Youth Aliyah, an organization that saved close to

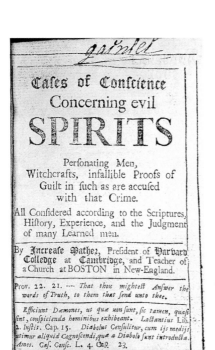

gauntlet

Cases of Conscience
Concerning evil
SPIRITS

Perfonating Men,
Witchcrafts, infallible Proofs of
Guilt in fuch as are accufed
with that Crime.

All Confidered according to the Scriptures,
Hiftory, Experience, and the Judgment
of many Learned men.

By **Increafe Mather**, Prefident of **Harvard
Colledge** at **Cambridge**, and Teacher of
a Church at BOSTON in New-England.

Prov. 22. 21. ---- *That thou mighteft Anfwer the
words of Truth, to them that fend unto thee.*

*Efficiunt Dæmones, ut quæ non funt, fic tamen, quafi
fint, confpicienda hominibus exhibeant. Lactantius Lib.
2. Inftit. Cap. 15. Diabolus Confulitur, cum ijs mediis
utimur aliquid Cognofcendi, quæ a Diabolo funt introducta.
Ames. Caf. Confc. L. 4. Cap. 23.*

BOSTON Printed, and Sold by *Benjamin
Harris* at the London Coffee-Houfe. 1693.

This flier announced the publication of a book about the evil that witches were believed to cause. In the 1693 book Increase Mather, the president of Harvard College, warned New Englanders that witches lived in their midst.

Women found guilty of witchcraft are being executed in this 1655 illustration. Thirty-five convicted witches died in colonial New England, of whom twenty-eight were female and seven were male.

Jarena Lee became the first nationally known African-American woman preacher. Her sermons inspired men and women, whites as well as blacks.

Harriet Beecher Stowe wrote the best-selling book of the nineteenth century, *Uncle Tom's Cabin*. In Stowe's sentimental novel the experience of a mother's love is the surest path to Christian faith.

Presbyterian missionaries approach an Apache woman on a reservation in Oklahoma in 1898. Missionaries believed that Christianity improved the status of women.

A crowd gathers outside Mary Baker Eddy's home for her welcome address. Every Christian Science service includes a reading from Eddy's book, *Science and Health with Key to the Scriptures*.

Florida women participate in a temperance parade. Female members of the WCTU saw public activism as an extension of their duties as mothers and wives.

Pentecostal preacher Aimee Semple McPherson once wowed congregants at her Angelus Temple in Los Angeles with a dramatic sermon entitled "Stop! You're Under Arrest!" Appearing on a motorcycle in front of the congregation, McPherson warned her hearers that they were speeding down the wrong avenues of life.

African-American women deliver food baskets to needy members of their community. In the late nineteenth and early twentieth centuries thousands of women organized religious groups to address social needs.

Female voices have predominated in church choirs throughout the United States, including that of the Japanese American First Evangelical Church, San Francisco, in 1940.

In this 1978 photograph, anti-ERA (Equal Rights Amendment) lobbyists pass the word to state legislators. Support for conservative values has grown along with the prevalence of fundamentalist religious groups.

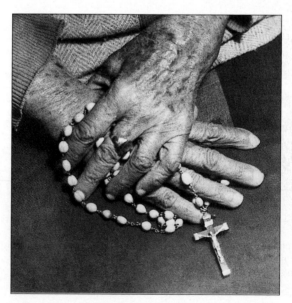

Rosa Cosilla displays her rosary, a string of beads used by Catholics in reciting prayers. Prayer helped many Catholic women cope with the hardships of immigration.

A woman admires a mural painted on the wall of a San Antonio housing project in the 1970s. She is looking at Our Lady of Guadalupe,
patron saint of Mexico.

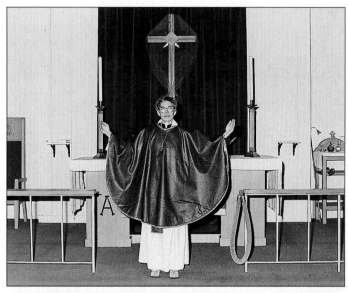

In addition to being a civil rights lawyer and the first African American to earn a Ph.D. from Yale Law School, Pauli Murray was the first African-American woman to be ordained an Episcopal priest. Here she is celebrating mass in 1978.

Jewish women read the Torah (sacred scripture) in a 1990s religious service. While Orthodox Jews still ban females from full synagogue participation, women now fill leadership roles in both Reform and Conservative congregations.

one hundred thousand European Jewish children by resettling them in Palestine.

Like Protestant missionary societies, Hadassah emphasized the connections between American women and those of a distant land, and it appealed to their compassion for the less fortunate. Just as returning missionaries toured the country giving firsthand accounts of conditions abroad, Hadassah officers and workers showed pictures of children in Palestine with flies swarming on their eyes and of the unsanitary conditions in which mothers gave birth. Most important, Hadassah mirrored the women's missionary groups in stressing the intellectual and spiritual benefits to members of helping women and children in another country. "We need Zionism as much as those Jews do who need a physical home," Henrietta Szold said of American women, including herself.

In spite of all these similarities, a fundamental difference separated Hadassah from the missionary movement. Christians hoped to convert those they planned to help. Jewish women, in contrast, were trying to improve the conditions of members of their own faith. Whether in the United States or in Palestine, Jews were part of a minority faith, and as Adolf Hitler's plan to exterminate the Jews of Europe progressed in the 1930s, the establishment of a Jewish state appeared more and more critical. This gave Zionism an urgency shared by few social movements and prompted a stunning proportion of American Jewish women to join Hadassah.

The early women Zionists were visionary idealists who worked to gain equal rights both for Jews without a country and for women. They envisioned a binational state of Arabs and Jews in Palestine that would be a model to the world of justice and cooperation. Their frank acknowledgment of the presence and dire conditions of the non-Jewish majority in Palestine sometimes separated them from male leaders, who were more focused on achieving the political rights of Jews. They believed American Jewish women needed the inspiration and education offered by the Zionist movement because there was little role for them in American Judaism.

Unlike Christian churches, American synagogues in the early twentieth century discouraged women's participation in lay activities. Henrietta Szold, herself deeply religious, bemoaned the lack of religious education available to American girls. She saw Hadassah as a way for women to increase their involvement both in their religion and in public life. "The Zionist organization," according to Szold, "since it believes in the equality of men and women, must educate Jewish women not only to Judaism but to a realization of their civic and national responsibilities."

Hadassah survived as a single-sex organization long after most Jews abandoned the idea that men and women should inhabit separate spheres. Although it was composed exclusively of women, it did not stress the concept of "women's work for women" to the same extent as earlier groups. Instead, it provided health care and education for all Jewish residents of Palestine, and it stressed its members' common interests with Jews of other countries rather than just with women. In addition, sex segregation continued to work in Jewish organizations because Judaism itself continued to separate men and women, giving women little role in synagogue worship. By the mid-twentieth century, synagogues would catch up to the reality of American conditions, in which women played a substantial role in religious institutions. Except among the orthodox, barriers between men and women came down, and women became the equals of the male laity. But before this, many American women expressed their identity as Jews through a passionate commitment to Zionism.

In some ways, the Jewish community benefited from the continued separation of men and women. While the men of the Zionist Organization of America (ZOA) argued over politics and ideology, Hadassah took up the practical work of building a new nation. Infighting and political struggles led to a decrease in the membership of the men's organization during the 1930s, but Hadassah continued to grow. During that crucial decade, in which much of the world tried to ignore increasing anti-Semitism, membership in Hadassah consistently outnumbered that of the ZOA by two to one. The women's insistence on using volunteer or low-paid workers contributed to the success of their fund-raising goals, while the ZOA went into debt. Although men's membership in Zionist organizations increased in the 1940s, the emergency of settling refugees from Nazi death camps and then fighting a war to secure Israel's independence required the support of all Jews, and women's work was not discouraged.

In the way that religious women have always conveyed values to their children, members of Hadassah cultivated their children's involvement in Zionist activities. Through their efforts, in part, support for Israel became a central feature of American Jewish identity as well as an element of U.S. foreign policy. Like the temperance movement, the missionary movement, and the work of Catholic sisters, Hadassah was one organization through which women's religious commitments influenced public affairs.

In the past (and in current Orthodox practice) Jewish women were not allowed to participate in the minyan, the quorum of ten men required for public prayer. The kaddish, recited to commemorate the anniversary of the death of a family member, is one such public prayer. Because only men could say kaddish, wives and daughters were represented in the minyan by male members of the community, and women were thereby denied direct participation in this rite of mourning. Henrietta Szold, the founder of Hadassah, the Women's Zionist Organization of America, responded by letter to a male friend of the family who volunteered to say kaddish for her mother.

New York, September 16, 1916

[To Haym Peretz]

It is impossible for me to find words in which to tell you how deeply I was touched by your offer to act as "*Kaddish*" for my dear mother. I cannot even thank you—it is something that goes beyond thanks. It is beautiful, what you have offered to do—I shall never forget it.

You will wonder, then, that I cannot accept your offer. Perhaps it would be best for me not to try to explain to you in writing, but to wait until I see you to tell you why it is so. I know well, and appreciate what you say about, the Jewish custom; and Jewish custom is very dear and sacred to me. And yet I cannot ask you to say *Kaddish* after my mother. The *Kaddish* means to me that the survivor publicly and markedly manifests his wish and intention to assume the relation to the Jewish community which his parent had, and that so the chain of tradition remains unbroken from generation to generation, each adding its own link. You can do that for the generations of your family, I must do that for the generations of my family.

I believe that the elimination of women from such duties was never intended by our law and custom—women were freed from positive duties when they could not perform them, but not when they could. It was never intended that, if they could perform them, their performance of them should not be considered as valuable and valid as when one of the male sex performed them. And of the *Kaddish* I feel sure this is particularly true.

My mother had eight daughters and no son; and yet never did I hear a word of regret pass the lips of either my mother or my father that one of us was not a son. When my father died, my mother would not permit others to take her daughters' place in saying the *Kaddish*, and so I am sure I am acting in her spirit when I am moved to decline your offer. But beautiful your offer remains nevertheless, and, I repeat, I know full well that it is much more in consonance with the generally accepted Jewish tradition than is my or my family's conception. You understand me, don't you?

CHAPTER 5

Old Faiths in New Times

"**W**omen are becoming ever more conscious of their human dignity," Pope John XXIII declared in 1963. "They will not tolerate being treated as mere material instruments, but demand rights befitting a human person both in domestic and public life," he wrote. Women's organizations had made extraordinary contributions to churches and synagogues during the first half of the twentieth century, but it was not until the 1960s that women began to ask for an equal say in the institutions sustained by their efforts. "The times they are a-changin'" sang Bob Dylan in 1963, and this was as true of religion as any other part of American life. Issues involving the role of women would be among the greatest challenges facing religious groups in the second half of the twentieth century. At the same time, America's religious landscape was changing. The decade of the 1960s saw the end of legal quotas that had previously prevented entry to the United States from most countries with non-Christian populations. As a result, the new social environment greeted an increasingly diverse religious population. Women from almost every religion in the world encountered the possibilities of life in modern America.

From 1963 to 1965, Pope John XXIII convened the Second Vatican Council (Vatican II), in which bishops assembled from around the world to consider changes needed to bring the Catholic Church up to date. This was an unusual departure for a church that emphasized tradition and obedience to religious authority. "Every type of discrimination, whether social or cultural, whether based on sex, race, color, social condition, language, or religion, is to be overcome and eradicated as contrary to God's intent," the bishops declared. They explicitly recognized the rights of women to "equity with men in law and in fact." It seemed clear that they meant to encourage new roles for women both in the church and in the larger society. For women who felt conflicts between the new emphasis on equality and traditional Catholic teachings about their role, the era of Vatican II was one of hope and possibility.

The bishops who assembled in Rome were, of course, all men. Only ordained priests participate in the formulation of Catholic teachings, and only men can be ordained. At the council's second session, Cardinal Léon Joseph Suenens of Belgium said, "In our age, when woman goes almost to the moon, it is indispensable that she play a more important role in the church." He proposed admitting women as auditors to the council. Twenty-two women were invited to listen to the three thousand male participants, but they were not permitted to speak or to vote.

An American woman who had not been invited traveled to Rome to witness the historic council. Mary Daly was already in Europe, studying at the University of Fribourg, in Switzerland. She wanted to attain the Catholic Church's highest level of theological learning, a doctorate in sacred theology from a pontifical faculty authorized directly by the Vatican. She already had a doctorate in theology from Notre Dame, but the only school in the United States that conferred the pontifical degree—Catholic University of America in Washington, D.C.—refused to admit her because she was female. Daly then applied to the University of Fribourg, because the state-sponsored university was not permitted to exclude women. There she became the first woman ever to receive the doctorate in sacred theology from a pontifical faculty. Still eager to learn, she earned a second doctorate at Fribourg in philosophy.

During the Second Vatican Council, Daly spent a month in Rome. She borrowed a press pass to observe debates on church doctrine and policy. She watched the red-robed cardinals read speeches in Latin. The handful of women who had been admitted as auditors, mostly veiled nuns, silently knelt and bowed their heads to receive communion from the men. A few of the bishops joined Cardinal Suenens to insist that the council address the status of women and argued that bringing the church up to date meant an expanded role for women. Daly left Rome with the conviction that women were second-class citizens in Catholicism but also that Vatican II marked the beginning of a new era of openness in which change was possible. She returned to the United States to join the theology faculty at Boston College.

In 1968 Daly published *The Church and the Second Sex*, which outlined the contradictions she saw between Catholic teachings about women and the church's assertion of equal respect for the dignity of all human beings. The book proposed reforms to end discrimination against women, such as including girls as altar servers, allowing women's orders more autonomy from bishops and priests, ending prohibitions on birth control, and rejecting theological traditions that present women as spiritually inferior to men. The book marked a watershed in the engagement of religion and feminism, the new movement aimed at securing the political, social, and economic equality of women.

Daly's book made her an instant celebrity because of its controversial challenges to an apparently unmovable institution. At Boston College, the book led to her dismissal. Its criticism of the Catholic Church's treatment of women was shocking to many and unacceptable at a Catholic institution. But it was in harmony with the tone of American culture in 1969, which applauded change in general and the principle of self-determination in particular. After mass student protests and a public outcry, Daly was reinstated. The experience changed her views, however, and Daly gave up on the Catholic Church. She concluded that a negative view of women was embedded in the fundamental doctrines of Christianity. A religion centered on a male deity as creator, judge, and savior, she now believed, could never include women as equal participants. In 1973 she declared herself a "post-Christian feminist" and published *Beyond God the Father: Toward a Philosophy of Women's Liberation*. Christianity, Daly now claimed, could not be reformed.

Daly's books represent two alternative reactions to the encounter between religion and the quest for women's rights. The first response was a desire to reform religious institutions in order to improve women's status within them; the second was to abandon those institutions as inherently oppressive to women. A third strategy, which Daly did not consider, was to accept traditional religious teachings about women as part of God's plan and use them to criticize changes in society that have diminished the difference between men's and women's roles. All three of these responses have attracted large numbers of American women.

Since the 1960s, the ordination of women has been one of the most important goals for those who believe that Christianity and Judaism should be reformed so that women and men receive equal treatment. Today, when women serve in almost every profession, it is perhaps difficult to recapture the symbolic impact of women's entry into the male preserve of the ministry. The priest or pastor represented both social and divine order when he stood before his congregation, leading them in devotions and helping them to know the will of God. The idea that a woman might assume this role represented a shocking reversal of traditional roles, one that is still objectionable to many Americans.

Although a few women throughout history, like the African-American preacher Jarena Lee, followed the call to preach, in most cases they did so without the official recognition of their churches in the form of ordination. In 1853, Antoinette Brown (later Blackwell) became the first woman formally ordained to the Christian ministry in a recognized denomination. After graduating from Oberlin College, she was called by a small Congregationalist church in South Butler, New York. Because Congregationalism allows each congregation to select its own minister, the South Butler church was able to ordain Brown without consulting the rest of the denomination. By the end of the nineteenth century, a small number of women had been ordained in Congregationalist churches and other denominations that select ministers without wider church authorization (Baptists, Disciples of Christ, Christian, Unitarians, and Universalists).

In denominations requiring more formal authorization for ordination, the movement of women into the ministry was more difficult. This was just one of the many issues that had to be negotiated in American Protestantism's complicated history. As various groups split off from each other or united along ethnic, theological, political, or sectional lines, women's rights rose and fell within the churches, often sacrificed to denominational unity. Liberal splinter groups among Methodists and Presbyterians ordained women toward the end of the nineteenth century. When the Methodists reunited in 1939, they reached a compromise in which they accepted women as local preachers but denied them full recognition as voting members of the denomination's governing bodies. Both Methodists and northern Presbyterians, however, gave women full ordination rights in 1956.

Before the 1970s, whether or not a church ordained women made little difference. Prevailing attitudes about women's lack of capacity for leadership meant that few women sought ordination anyway. Women constituted less than 3 percent of ordained clergy. The majority of these were in the Holiness and Pentecostal churches that sprang up around the turn of the century. These churches accepted women's leadership not out of concern for equality but because they paid more attention to the movement of the Holy Spirit than to church order. The larger Holiness churches (Church of the Nazarene, Salvation Army, Church of God) had, in fact, split off from the Methodists in hope of returning to the spirit-inspired roots of their faith. In defense of women's ministry, they pointed to biblical texts describing women preaching in the time of Jesus. They often referred to the prophet Joel's declaration that as the Final Judgment approached, God would pour out his spirit on both men and women, "and thy sons and thy daughters shall prophesy" (Joel 2:28).

Many Pentecostal churches allow the ordination of women, despite the belief of most of their members that the Bible teaches traditional roles for women and men. Because women predominate in speaking in tongues, some naturally rise to leadership positions in groups that respect this religious practice. Even though some church members cite Paul's biblical injunctions against women preaching and teaching to keep denominational leadership in the hands of men, others point to texts that support women's ministry. Pentecostal women ministers frequently agree with church teachings suggesting that a woman's primary role should be that of wife and mother and that, in general, women should not aspire to leadership in the church. Individual women, however, often feel that they have been called to preach in spite of their sex and that they must respond.

The emphasis on inspired, charismatic leadership in Pentecostalism allowed a number of women to start new denominations that reflected their highly individual leadership styles. Aimee Semple McPherson's theatrical entrances to worship services are a good example. She once rode a motorcycle onto the stage of her Angelus Temple in Los Angeles. Because the largest African-American Pentecostal denomination, the Church of God in Christ, officially bars women from ordination as elders or ministers, black women who have felt called to preach have often served independent congregations, sometimes of their own founding.

As Holiness and Pentecostal churches have become more institutionalized and have established colleges and seminaries, the proportion of women ministers has decreased. The number of women clergy in the Church of the Nazarene dropped from 20 percent in 1908 to 1 percent in 1989. In the Church of God 32 percent of pastors were women in 1925 but only 15 percent were by 1992.

As the women's movement in the late 1960s gained power, campaigns for the ordination of women began both in religious groups in which it was formally possible but rarely done and in those that forbade it. These campaigns marked a new departure in religious history because they used structures of denominations to promote rather than block women's leadership.

In Christianity, the debate over the ordination of women cuts to the heart of the central doctrines of the faith—the nature of God and Christ. In the Roman Catholic, Episcopal, and Orthodox churches priests are understood to be Christ's direct representatives on earth. The sacrament of ordination connects them through an unbroken line of succession back to Jesus through his apostles. Their ability to administer the sacraments—for example, to turn bread and wine into the body and blood of Christ during Holy Communion—depends on their ritual ordination. Because Christ was male, can a woman represent Christ to the congregation? Those who believe that she cannot argue that when God took human form in the person of Jesus, maleness was essential to his role as savior to humanity. Those who believe that she can view Jesus' maleness as an incidental human attribute, not part of his divine nature. What was significant about Jesus, they argue, was that God became human, not that he became male.

The Episcopal Church began discussing women's ordination in 1919. Periodic reports of study commissions repeatedly concluded that there was no theological barrier to women's ordination but neither was there a theological necessity for it. In 1970, the church approved the consecration of women as deacons, a rite that, for men, usually preceded becoming a priest. But in the same year, the church's clerics voted against ordaining women as priests. In response, a group of laywomen, seminary students, and women deacons organized a women's caucus to argue for the ordination of women. When the House of Bishops voted to form yet another committee to study the question, the women's caucus objected, saying that no more study was needed. They refused to cooperate, and the bishops could not find any Episcopal women willing to join the committee. At the 1973 general convention, women's ordination was rejected once again, this time in a close vote.

Alla Bozarth-Campbell, ordained as a deacon in 1971, was one of the women waiting to be ordained as a priest as soon as a positive vote occurred. Like other members of the women's caucus, she was devastated by the second negative vote in 1973. When her husband was consecrated as a priest in 1974, she stood in the doorway at the back of the church. When her husband responded to the bishop's examination, she responded, too. As the bishop and other priests laid their hands on the new priest, a deacon, one priest, and a dozen women moved to the back of the church to join her, to show their conviction that her ordination should be as valid as her husband's.

Later that year, Bozarth-Campbell became part of a group of eleven women deacons who decided to seek ordination without the full sanction of their church. After so many delays, they felt they could not wait another three years until the church's next general convention, with no promise that they would be ordained even then. Three retired bishops agreed to ordain them on the Feast of Saints Mary and Martha (July 29) at the Church of the Advocate in North Philadelphia. The eleven women released a letter saying, "We are certain God needs women in the priesthood to be true to the Gospel understanding of human unity in Christ." Their primary motivation, they wrote, was to "free the priesthood from the bondage it suffers as long as it is characterized by the categorical exclusion of persons on the basis of sex."

Bishop John Allin, the head of the Episcopal Church in the United States, sent a telegram begging the women to abandon their plans, but the service proceeded as scheduled. It was interrupted when the presiding bishop said, "If there be any of you who knoweth any impediment or notable crime (in these women), let him come forward in the name of God." Several priests came forward and read statements opposing the ordination of women. But the presiding bishops said they were acting in obedience to God. "Hearing his command, we can heed no other. The time for our obedience is now," they said, and proceeded with the ordination.

The House of Bishops quickly condemned the irregular ordinations. But the Episcopal Divinity School in Cambridge, Massachusetts, ignored the bishops and offered faculty appointments with full priestly duties to two of the eleven women. There they celebrated Holy Communion with the rest of the ordained faculty. Many feared the church would be torn apart if it did not ordain women, and others threatened to leave it if it did. When the question of women priests came up at the 1976 general convention, the delegates debated for four hours. Then they rose for five minutes of silent prayer before voting. Both clerical and lay delegates approved the ordination of women by a wide margin. There was stunned silence in the convention hall.

The Episcopal Church's decision to ordain women did not, however, end the controversy over women priests. Bishop Allin announced his conscientious inability to accept women as priests and offered his resignation. Many other church members were also unable to overcome their reservations. They had grown up thinking of the priest's maleness as part of his similarity to Christ, and they felt uncomfortable receiving the sacraments from a woman. About 5 percent of members left the church over this decision.

By 2000, more than two thousand women were Episcopal priests, some 13 percent of the total, and equal numbers of men and women were ordained that year. The bishops demonstrated their broad acceptance of the ordination of women by electing the Reverend Katharine Jefferts Schori to lead the church as presiding bishop in 2006. While heralded as a show of unity on women's status in the church in the United States, the election of Bishop Jefferts Schori highlighted differences between Americans and their co-religionists in the Anglican Communion, the world's largest communion of Protestants, most of whose members reside in Africa. At the 2007 meeting of presiding bishops, six refused to share communion with Bishop Jefferts Schori. They explained this unusual action by calling attention to the fact that she, like most American bishops, supported the ordination of a gay priest as bishop of New Hampshire. However, it is notable that none of these bishops ordain women in their own churches.

About half of all American religious groups currently ordain women. The largest number of women clergy (4,370 in 2000) serve the United Methodist Church, with large numbers ordained by Presbyterian, Lutheran, and Baptist bodies as well as by the Disciples of Christ. Reform Jews voted to ordain women as rabbis in 1972, and Conservative Jews in 1985.

But the country's largest religious groups, the Catholic Church and the Southern Baptist Convention, have firmly rejected women's ordination. When other groups that ordain only men are added (Mormons, the Church of God in Christ, Missouri Synod Lutherans, Seventh-day Adventists, Muslims, Orthodox Christians, and Orthodox Jews, for example), most religious Americans probably worship in congregations where women are not eligible for the ministry.

The Episcopal understanding of the priesthood closely resembles Catholic and Orthodox Christian views, so observers wondered if their decision to ordain women would be followed by similar moves in those churches. In the Catholic Church, Vatican II had already prompted calls for women's ordination. In 1974, superiors of Catholic women's orders unanimously endorsed the opening of all forms of ministry to women. The Women's Ordination Conference formed to advocate for women priests. But the Vatican's apparent openness on the subject has given way to increasingly firm refusals. In 1977 it published a *Declaration on the Question of the Admission of Women to Ministerial Priesthood*. In it women's ordination was rejected on the basis of Jesus' example.

He chose only men as his apostles, even though he departed from convention in many other instances. Thus, the declaration explained, he must have intended to limit the priesthood to men, and Catholics must follow his example. In 1994 Pope John Paul II stated, "The church has no authority whatsoever to confer ordination on women and this judgment is to be definitely held by all the church's faithful." The final phrase suggests that the letter was intended to close the thirty-year debate on this subject, but it stops just short of declaring the rejection of women as priests to be an infallible teaching. Attempts to ordain Catholic women outside of canon law have met with excommunications and harsh renunciations from Rome.

The majority of American Catholics, however, support the ordination of women and believe that priests should be able to marry. This disagreement with official teaching mirrors their rejection of the Church's prohibition on the use of birth control. The Vatican's prohibition on women priests has created a strange situation in the United States, where the church continues to grow but where the number of men wanting to be priests continues to decrease. Because of the shortage of priests, Catholic canon law has been amended to permit a layperson to provide "pastoral care" to a parish but not to administer sacraments such as Communion. As a result, women, including nuns, increasingly serve as leaders of parishes. In addition, about half of the nineteen thousand Catholic churches in the United States have women serving as nonordained, paid parish ministers. Under these conditions, many Catholics do not feel that their disagreement with the Vatican affects their worship experience.

Some Catholic women who once sought ordination now say that the priesthood is no longer their goal. After three decades of being told that women cannot be priests, they have concluded that the priesthood represents the hierarchical structure of traditional Catholicism, not the egalitarian Church they hoped would follow from Vatican II. Instead of the priesthood, they now seek the meaning of their faith in alternative communities of women, where the Bible is interpreted in light of people's experience. Known as Women-Church, this movement marks a shift in the stance of feminists toward the Catholic Church. Instead of petitioning the male power structure for permission to join its ranks, they seek to define the Church for themselves. In doing so, they believe they continue the spirit of Vatican II with its assertion that the people of God, rather than ecclesiastical structures, constitute the true Catholic Church.

Since the mid-1980s, there has been little movement on the ordination of women. In an unexpected move, the nation's largest Protestant denomination, the Southern Baptist Convention, voted to ban the practice in 1984, although local churches had occasionally ordained women since 1965. This move was especially surprising because it violated the Baptist principle of autonomy for individual congregations. The Baptists voted for the ban because the ordination of women was seen as conflicting with a literal interpretation of the Bible.

Among Protestants, objections to the ordination of women center on biblical texts supporting the idea of male headship. According to this view, when God created Adam first, and then created Eve to be his helpmate, he established the order of creation—God is the head of Christ, Christ is the head of man, and man is the head of woman (1 Corinthians 11:2–5). The 1984 Southern Baptist Statement on Women's Ordination notes that the Apostle Paul excludes women from pastoral leadership "to preserve a submission God requires because the man was first in creation and the woman was first in the Edenic Fall." The statement reiterates the Baptist principle of the final authority of Scripture in matters of Christian faith and cautions against the influence of modern social practices on Christian doctrine. By using the idea of "male headship," it also suggests that literal interpretations of the Bible may call for women's subservience to men in many areas beyond the issue of ordination.

As the Southern Baptist example shows, the issue of the ordination of women cannot be separated from a religious group's general beliefs about appropriate roles for men and women, or from its basic religious doctrines. Ordination, it turns out, is only the tip of the iceberg. In many traditions women are discovering new ways to translate and interpret their scriptures, new words to refer to God, and even new conclusions about the nature of God's relationship to human beings. These concerns have inspired a blossoming of new explorations in the areas of scriptural studies, history, religious ethics, and theology, as well as a burst of creativity in redesigning religious rituals.

Jewish and Christian feminists take as their point of departure the account of human origins in Genesis 1:26: "So God created man in his own image...male and female created he them." They argue that if females are created in the image of God, this means that God has imparted a divine nature to men and women equally, making them both capable of all spiritual attainments. A God who is as concerned with the personhood and redemption of women as with that of men would not create a tradition that subjugates women to men. This, feminists assert, is an essential religious truth, and other texts and doctrines must be interpreted in ways that do not contradict it.

Christians find New Testament support for this view in Paul's letter to the Galatians (Galatians 3:28): "There is neither Jew nor Greek, there is neither slave nor free, there is neither male nor female, for you are all one in Christ Jesus."

Like African-American liberation theologians—who believe that the core message of Christianity is one of liberation to the oppressed—Christian feminists believe that texts which seem to support subservience or inequality should be reinterpreted in light of the core message of the equality of all human persons. For example, Paul's instructions to the Corinthians that women should keep silent in church (1 Corinthians 15:34) can be questioned in many ways. The translation from the Greek can be challenged, so that the text is understood to prohibit only distracting speech that is not part of the worship service. Or Paul's motivation can be questioned, so that his statement is seen as a reflection of the prejudices of his time, rather than his role as Jesus' apostle. Or examples from other biblical texts can be offered as a corrective. Feminist scholars point to Paul's references to the deacon Phoebe, and to a woman named Junia, whom he calls "outstanding among the apostles," as examples of women who spoke in the early church, but whose voices have been buried by history.

Whether a denomination can tolerate advocates of women's equality among its believers depends on its view of the Bible. Denominations that acknowledge modern biblical criticism view the Bible as a divinely inspired document that was produced by fallible human beings who could not help but include the cultural assumptions and prejudices of their era. Feminist scholars assert that the Bible was written by men who incorporated sexist assumptions about women. But many churches disagree. They reject biblical criticism, viewing the Bible as divinely inspired in every word, and therefore never wrong. For these denominations, there is no room for reinterpretation. Biblical injunctions requiring women's subservience to men must be obeyed. Women in these religious groups accept such teachings as Paul's statement, "Wives, be subject to your husbands, as to the Lord" (Ephesians 5:22).

Some of the most significant challenges of feminist scholarship involve religious language. Traditional religions portray God as a masculine figure—Father, Lord, and King. Feminists counter that all language for God is metaphorical. Using exclusively masculine imagery for God, they assert, is idolatrous, because it substitutes a human characteristic (maleness) for the unknowable character of God. If women are truly created in the image of God as much as men are, feminists argue, then it is as appropriate to use feminine images and pronouns to refer to God as it is to use the more traditional masculine terms. They offer examples from Scripture and history that depict God as possessing attributes associated with mothers as well as fathers. Biblical texts compare God to a woman in labor (Isaiah 42:14), to a suckling mother (Numbers 11:12), and to a midwife (Isaiah 46:3–4). Some argue that images of God should be expanded beyond parental terms or those relating to secular authority (Lord, King). Simply to add feminine equivalents of these terms leaves the believer permanently in the role of child or subject. Some argue that images of friendship and partnership should join parental models of the human/divine relationship. Mary Daly suggested that we think of God as a verb, as a perpetual process of becoming, rather than as a completed object.

The use of feminine language for God continues to be controversial even among religious groups that have accepted other reforms relating to women. Two thousand Christian women gathered in Minneapolis to explore the use of feminine images in prayer and liturgy at the ecumenical Re-Imagining Conference in 1993. In one ceremony, they used the feminine term *Sophia*, the Greek word for "wisdom," to refer to "the feminine face of God." This provoked charges of heresy from conservative groups within the Methodist and Presbyterian churches.

For religious women who think that abandoning masculine God imagery is in fundamental conflict with the Jewish and Christian traditions, there are two alternatives. The millions of American women who sustain churches that take this position find that masculine images provide the most useful metaphors for understanding God. They accept God's masculinity as mirroring aspects of his divine nature as well as of the created order. A smaller, but not insignificant, group of women, has chosen a different path. They have abandoned their traditions altogether. Like Mary Daly, these women decided to replace the patriarchal deity with a feminine manifestation of the divine. They agree with theologian Carol Christ, who argued in her 1978 essay "Why Women Need the Goddess" that the symbol of the Goddess is needed to counteract the "devaluation of female power, denigration of the female body, distrust of female will, and the denial of women's bonds and heritage that have been engendered by patriarchal religion." A new movement of women's spirituality has emerged among those who have rejected established religions.

The goal of women's spirituality is to recover a connection among women, nature, and divine power believed to have been repressed during centuries of male-dominated religion. Participants reject the biblical creation story, in which a patriarchal deity first creates man, and then creates woman to help him. They see the story of Eve being created from Adam's rib as a reversal of the natural order, in which woman is the source of life who gives birth to all people. In place of the biblical creation, they look to a pre-monotheistic paradise when Goddess worship represented a reverence for nature and for women as givers of life. This idyllic matriarchal past is often depicted as a time before war, slavery, or the concentration of wealth, all of which are associated with the rise of male power. Religious practices of pre-Christian Europe are seen as a source of such beliefs, whose modern advocates are sometimes called "neo-pagans." Many participants call themselves witches. They feel a special identification with the thousands of women killed by Christian authorities during the witch hunts in Europe.

Proponents of women's spirituality see the Goddess as present throughout nature and in human women. They seek contact with the divine through rituals designed to encourage the experience of women's power. The Goddess is often invoked, but participants believe the power of the ritual comes as much from themselves as from a deity. Because women embody the Goddess, rituals are intended to promote self-discovery within a group of like-minded women. Some take as their motto the black poet Ntozake Shange's verse, "i found god in myself & i loved her / i loved her fiercely." Rituals frequently focus on life-cycle events such as menstruation, childbirth, and menopause. Chanting, dancing, or drumming generate energy, which can then be "sent" out for a specific purpose. Rituals are often spontaneous or unique events, aimed at encouraging individual creativity, which is believed to express divine female energy.

Women's spirituality is a diffuse movement. Most participants do not belong to any formal associations because they reject the hierarchical structures and organizations that have permitted other religious groups to restrict women's role. Some Christian and Jewish feminists view women's spirituality as a source of creative inspiration for their own attempts to reimagine God in nonsexist terms. Others are sharply critical of the movement for simply reversing the sexism of patriarchy and replacing it with matriarchy. They point out that there is no historical evidence that women enjoyed a higher status than men in pre-Christian goddess-worshipping societies. In fact, the archaeological record suggests that the power of the goddess was usually understood to bolster the authority of a male king or ruler. They also question the movement's focus on individual experience rather than on the good of the community.

Although some women have responded to the movement for women's equality by abandoning established faiths, others have responded by reaffirming their commitment to traditional religious roles. Women who see their roles as wives and mothers as the highest expression of their religious calling may find the new emphasis on equality problematic. They reject the idea that public roles traditionally assigned to men are more valuable or desirable than the private roles of women in the family. Many, ironically, have found public outlets for these views in successful political campaigns involving women's issues. In 1982 the Equal Rights Amendment (ERA), the proposed constitutional amendment that would have prohibited discrimination on the basis of sex, failed to achieve ratification largely as the result of the efforts of religiously conservative groups. Conservative religious women have also played an important role in the ongoing debate about the legality and morality of abortion. Groups with significantly different beliefs and historical enmity among them, such as Mormons, Catholics, and Southern Baptists, have been able to cooperate for the first time because of their shared opposition to abortion. Many religious women viewed both the ERA and the legalization of abortion as undermining a God-ordained distinctive role for women as wives and mothers.

The movement for expanded roles for women in religion and society occurred at the same time that the United States opened its doors to immigrant groups long barred from entry. Beginning with the Chinese Exclusion Act of 1882 and culminating with the Immigration Act of 1924, U.S. law ensured that most immigrants came from Europe. Those from predominantly Buddhist and Hindu countries were excluded completely. Like the women's movement, liberalized immigration laws passed in 1965 were inspired by the civil rights movement aimed at eliminating discrimination based on race, color, or creed.

Small communities of American Muslims, Hindus, and Buddhists swelled as the result of immigration from India, China, Vietnam, and other countries in Asia and Africa. The largest number of immigrants continued to come from predominantly Christian countries such as Mexico, the Philippines, and Poland, and the vast majority of religious Americans continue to practice Christianity. But most major cities now include at least one Buddhist temple, Hindu shrine, and Muslim mosque. Many also include places of worship of smaller religious groups such as Sikhs, Jains, and practitioners of indigenous religions from Africa and the Caribbean.

Like generations of immigrant women before them, those arriving after 1965 endeavored both to perpetuate the traditions of their homelands and to embrace the new opportunities America offered to women. Recently arrived groups mirror the model of most American religious organizations: men lead while women are the majority of practitioners. It can now be said that women form the backbone not only of the church but of the temple, shrine, and mosque as well. A 2004 study of Buddhist temples found that about twice as many women as men are regular participants—exactly the same gender ratio found in most Protestant churches. Also like Christian women, non-Christians often serve religious organizations in ways that extend domestic responsibilities of the home into the public sphere. In Buddist temples, for example, women have traditionally carried out the religious obligation of providing food on a daily basis for the monks who live at the temple. Women cannot enter monastic orders in the forms of Buddhism practiced by immigrants from Thailand, Laos, and Cambodia, so women's religious role centers on support for male monks. Yet, women in these groups have also assumed new religious roles, such as teaching and leading chanting or meditation.

With approximately five million followers in the United States, Islam will soon outdistance Judaism as America's largest non-Christian religion. Muslims in North America include immigrants from Asia, Africa, Eastern Europe, and the Middle East, as well as a substantial number of converts and children of converts, most of them African American. This last group has brought the experience of the predominantly Christian civil rights movement into the Muslim community. Living in the United States has increased women's participation in mosque worship and activities, which was discouraged or forbidden in some of the countries from which Muslims came. These religious activists join an international trend of increased quranic study and religious inquiry among Muslim women.

Like Christian feminists, egalitarian Muslims question whether traditional limitations on women's role are part of the central teachings of their faith or whether they have been added by male interpreters. At the same time, immigrant families may find the lack of modesty and respect for American women startling. They question whether the exploitation of women's sexuality in advertising and entertainment should be seen as "liberating." Young Muslim women in the United States may wear a *hijab*, or head covering, as an expression of religious and ethnic pride, one that is adopted as a free choice in a multireligious society, as well as an observance of the Muslim value of modesty. The descision of young Americans to wear the *hijab* can be as surprising to their more assimilated parents as it is to non-Muslim neighbors and co-workers. Just as each immigrant group, from Puritans to Catholics and Jews, has both adapted their faith to the United States and added something to American culture, Muslims now participate in secular American educational and cultural institutions, as well as founding distinctive schools, mosques, and community centers to perpetuate their traditions.

The opening of the twenty-first century has seen women step into visible leadership roles in the Muslim community. In 2001 Chereffe Kadri was elected president of the Islamic Society of Greater Toledo, Ohio, probably the first woman ever to lead a mosque community. That same year Ingrid Matson was elected vice president of the Islamic Society of North America, the largest Muslim organization in the United States. The society elected her as its president in 2006.

Islam has no formal ordination process, so women have been able to step into new roles based on their work as scholars of Muslim law. Shamshad Sheik, who earned a degree in Islamic law before coming to the United States from Pakistan, was appointed associate chaplain at Yale University in 2007. Sister Shamshad, as she prefers to be called, addresses the needs not only of Muslim students, but also of Buddhists, Sihks, Baha'is, Hindus, and Zoroastrians.

Other women scholars have broken boundaries by performing wedding ceremonies, and, most notably, by leading Friday prayers, the weekly religious service in mosques. This signal event occurred on March 18, 2005, when Amina Wadud, associate professor of Islamic studies at Virginia Commonwealth University, led the weekly Friday prayers for a mixed group of one hundred Muslim men and women in New York City. The departure from tradition sent shockwaves throughout the Muslim world, but many participants felt it was overdue. "A burden inside me had been lifted in the days after the prayer, and for weeks afterward I walked around New York consumed by a lightness I had never quite felt before," recalled one female attendee.

Although women's leadership has great symbolic significance, most Muslim women, like women in any religious group,
are more affected on a daily basis by the impact of their religion
on marriage, family, and personal life. Organizations of Muslim
women often focus on using Islamic law to defend women's
rights. The Muslim Women's League, for example, takes as its
mission "to implement the values of Islam and thereby reclaim
the status of women as free, equal and vital contributors to society." Its members view practices harmful to women in Muslim
societies—violence against women, rape, and honor killings,
for example—as the result of misinterpretation of the Quran
or ignorance of its teachings. Religious literacy, in their view, is
the best tool women have to promote their rights. Their programs seek to fight discrimination against Muslim women both
as Muslims and as women.

Many members of other religious groups face similar issues.
Women settling in the United States from Asia, the Carribean,
Latin America, or Africa may find it difficult to tell where religious discrimination ends and ethnic or racial discimination
begins. They sometimes face a double bind of needing to defend
their ethnic community from attack at the same time that they
criticize inequality within it. While women in non-Christian
religious groups experience the openness of American society,
they do so in a religious landscape deeply divided over wom-
en's issues. Since the mid-1960s, the fastest growing religious
groups in the United States have been those that take a conservative position on women's role. Most of these emphasize
homemaking and child rearing as God-given roles for women,
do not ordain women, and view women's subservience to men
as mandated by the bible. These groups include relatively recent
organizations of fundamentalist and Pentecostal Christians as
well as groups trying to perpetuate a centuries-old way of life in

isolated communities, such as the Amish and the Hasidic Jews, and religions of recent immigrants trying to perpetuate the values of their homelands.

Yet the same years that have seen conservative religions grow have also seen dramatic shifts toward egalitarian religious practices and unprecedented strides for women in religious leadership. Groups that do not ordain women have had to prove that they do not discriminate against women and that they value their religious service. Not only are women ordained in dozens of groups that did not do so fifty years ago, but they have been elected to lead several important Protestant denominations. In 2000, the Reverend Dr. Vashti McKenzie was elected the first woman bishop in the two-hundred-year history of the African Methodist Episcopal Church. She was elected president of the council of bishops, becoming the titular head of the church, in 2003, and was joined by two other women bishops in 2004. The following year the General Assembly of the Christian Church (Disciples of Christ) elected Sharon E. Watkins to be the denomination's first woman general minister and president. The success of these figures as well as Episcopal bishop Katharine Jefferts Schori presents a stark contrast to the continued exclusion of women from the highest levels of leadership in many religious settings.

Whether a religious organization is recently arrived, long established, or home grown, its views about women are among the most important signs of where it sits on the spectrum of American social outlooks. Some have embraced new roles for women, ordaining them to the ministry, revising prayer books and liturgies to reflect the shared humanity of women and men, and encouraging egalitarian scriptural criticism and theological reflection. Other groups have rejected change, seeing women's leadership as a threat to religious teachings and to the distinctive roles of men and women ordained by God. Religious views continue to shape deeply held beliefs about appropriate roles for women. As young women shape a new world in the twenty-first century, they navigate complicated spiritual terrain.

Religion can be a source of strength, identity, wisdom and autonomy, or it can be a challenge to women's aspirations for themselves, their daughters, and their communities. But one thing is clear: this relatively young country provides an environment in which women choose to play unprecedented roles in ancient faiths, as well as to uphold treasured traditions. If the pattern of American history holds, it will be women's choices that determine the future of religion in the United States.

In some Islamic countries such as Iran and Saudi Arabia, strict dress codes for women, including the wearing of the chador (a tent-like black cloth or veil), are enforced by the state. In other countries Muslim women, especially university-educated, urban women, voluntarily wear a variety of veils or head-coverings in order to show support for Islamic culture. Though veiling is technically not a religious require- ment, it does fulfill the Islamic law to dress modestly in public, a law that applies to both men and women. For many women, modest Mus- lim dress has practical advantages as well as cultural meaning. In the following article, Naheed Mustafa, a twenty-one-year-old Cana- dian college student, explains her decision to adopt the hijab (literally "drape," "cover," "partition") in 1993.

[W]hy would I, a woman with all the advantages of a North American upbringing, suddenly, at twenty-one, want to cover myself so that with the *hijab* and the other clothes I choose to wear, only my face and hands show?

Because it gives me freedom.

Women are taught from early childhood that their worth is proportional to their attractiveness. We feel compelled to pur- sue abstract notions of beauty, half realizing that such a pursuit is futile.

When women reject this form of oppression, they face rid- icule and contempt. Whether it's women who refuse to wear makeup or to shave their legs or to expose their bodies, society, both men and women, have trouble dealing with them.

In the Western world, the *hijab* has come to symbolize either forced silence or radical, unconscionable militancy. Actually, it's neither. It is simply a woman's assertion that judgment of her physical person is to play no role whatsoever in social interaction.

Wearing the *hijab* has given me freedom from constant atten-tion to my physical self. Because my appearance is not subjected to public scrutiny, my beauty, or perhaps lack of it, has been removed from the realm of what can legitimately be discussed.

No one knows whether my hair looks as if I just stepped out of a salon, whether or not I can pinch an inch, or even if I have unsightly stretch marks. And because no one knows, no one cares.

Feeling that one has to meet the impossible male stand-ards of beauty is tiring and often humiliating. I should know, I spent my entire teenage years trying to do it. I was a borderline bulimic and spent a lot of money I didn't have on potions and lotions in hopes of becoming the next Cindy Crawford.

The definition of beauty is ever-changing; waifish is good, waifish is bad, athletic is good—sorry, athletic is bad. Narrow hips? Great. Narrow hips? Too bad.

Women are not going to achieve equality with the right to bare their breasts in public, as some people would like to have you believe. That would only make us party to our own objecti-fication. True equality will be had only when women don't need to display themselves to get attention and won't need to defend their decision to keep their bodies to themselves.

CHRONOLOGY

1531

Our Lady of Guadalupe appears to Juan Diego, a Christian Indian, in Mexico

1619

First enslaved Africans arrive in the British colony of Virginia

1631

Margaret Winthrop arrives in Massachusetts

1634

Anne Hutchinson arrives in Massachusetts; she is banished in 1638

1692

Salem, Massachusetts, witch trials

1774

Ann Lee establishes the United Society of Believers in Christ's Second Appearing, called Shakers

1811

Jarena Lee, a member of the African Methodist Episcopal Church, is called to preach

1812

Elizabeth Seton founds the Sisters of Charity in Baltimore

1821–35

Evangelical revivals encourage women's testimony and reform activities

1834

New York Female Moral Reform Society founded

1848

Kate and Margaret Fox hear mysterious rappings on the walls and floor of the family farmhouse in Hydesville, New York, beginning the movement of Spiritualism

1852

Harriet Beecher Stowe publishes *Uncle Tom's Cabin*

1853

Antoinette Brown Blackwell is ordained to the Congregational clergy

1874

Founding of the Woman's Christian Temperance Union

1875

Mary Baker Eddy publishes *Science and Health*, establishing the faith of Christian Science

1890–1923

Three million Jews arrive in the United States from Russia and eastern Europe

1901

Alma White founds the Methodist Pentecostal Union in Colorado. In 1917 the name is changed to Pillar of Fire Church, headquartered in New Jersey

1912

Henrietta Szold founds Hadassah, the Women's Zionist Organization of America

1956

Methodist Episcopal Church and Presbyterian Church (USA) each ordain their first woman with full clergy rights

1963–65

Second Vatican Council

1965

Immigration Reform Act admits immigrants from countries with large Hindu, Buddhist, and Muslim populations

1970

Lutheran Church in America votes to ordain women

1972

Reform Jews vote to ordain women

1973

Mary Daly publishes *Beyond God the Father: Toward a Philosophy of Women's Liberation*

1976

Episcopal Church votes to ordain women

1984

Southern Baptist Convention votes to end the ordination of women

1985

Conservative Jews vote to ordain women

1998

Feminist Christians attend the fourth Re-Imagining conference in St. Paul to explore uses of feminine imagery and language in prayer and liturgy

2000

Rev. Dr. Vashti McKenzie elected first woman bishop in African Methodist Episcopal Church

2005

In New York City, Amina Wadud, associate professor of Islamic studies at Virginia Commonwealth University, is thought to be the first woman to lead Friday prayers for a group of Muslim men and women.

2006

Rev. Katharine Jefferts Schori elected presiding bishop of the Episcopal Church

FURTHER READING

GENERAL READING ON RELIGION IN THE UNITED STATES

Ahlstrom, Sidney. *A Religious History of the American People.* New Haven: Yale University Press, 1972.

Butler, Jon, and Harry S. Stout, eds. *Religion in American History: A Reader.* New York: Oxford University Press, 1997.

Gaustad, Edwin. *A Religious History of America.* Rev. ed. San Francisco: Harper & Row, 1990.

Marty, Martin. *Pilgrims in Their Own Land: 500 Years of Religion in America.* New York: Penguin, 1985.

AUTOBIOGRAPHIES AND BIOGRAPHIES

Abdul-Ghafur, Saleemah. *Living Islam Out Loud: American Muslim Women Speak.* Boston: Beacon Press, 2006.

Andrews, William L. *Sisters of the Spirit: Three Black Women's Autobiographies of the Nineteenth Century.* Bloomington: Indiana University Press, 1986.

Bacon, Margaret Hope. *Valiant Friend: The Life of Lucretia Mott.* New York: Walker, 1980.

Braude, Ann. *Transforming the Faiths of Our Fathers: Women Who Changed American Religion.* New York: Palgrave, 2005.

Cazden, Elizabeth. *Antoinette Brown Blackwell: A Biography.* Old Westbury, N.Y.: Feminist Press, 1983.

Dirvin, Joseph I. *Mrs. Seton, Foundress of the American Sisters of Charity.* New York: Farrar, Straus and Giroux, 1975.

Hedrick, Joan D. *Harriet Beecher Stowe: A Life.* New York: Oxford University Press, 1994.

Keller, Rosemary Skinner, and Rosemary Radford Ruether. *In Our Own Voices: Four Centuries of American Women's Religious Writing*. New York: HarperSanFrancisco, 1995.

Shaw, Anna Howard. *The Story of a Pioneer*. 1915. Reprint, Cleveland: Pilgrim Press, 1994.

Szold, Henrietta. *Lost Love: The Untold Story of Henrietta Szold: Unpublished Diaries and Letters*. Edited by Baila Round Shargel. Philadelphia: Jewish Publication Society, 1997.

Willard, Frances Elizabeth. *Writing Out My Heart: Selections from the Journal of Frances E. Willard, 1855–96*. Edited by Carolyn De Swarte Gifford. Urbana: University of Illinois Press, 1995.

Williams, Selma R. *Divine Rebel: The Life of Anne Marbury Hutchinson*. New York: Holt, Rinehart & Winston, 1981.

WOMEN AND RELIGION

Adler, Margot. *Drawing Down the Moon: Witches, Druids, Goddess-Worshippers, and Other Pagans in America Today*. Boston: Beacon Press, 1986.

Andrews, Edward Demming. *The People Called Shakers: A Search for the Perfect Society*. New York: Dover, 1963.

Anther, Joyce. *The Journey Home: How Jewish Women Shaped Modern America*. New York: Schocken, 1997.

Bacon, Margaret Hope. *Mothers of Feminism: The Story of Quaker Women in America*. San Francisco: Harper & Row, 1986.

Bushman, Claudia, ed. Mormon Sisters: Women in Early Utah. Logan: Utah State University Press, 1997.

Cadge, Wendy. *Heartwood: the First Generation of Theravada Buddhism in America*. Chicago: University of Chicago Press, 2005.

Daly, Mary. *The Church and the Second Sex, with the Feminist Post Christian Introduction and New Archaic Afterwords by the Author*. Boston: Beacon Press, 1985.

DeBerg, Betty A. *Ungodly Women: Gender and the First Wave of American Fundamentalism.* Minneapolis: Fortress Press, 1990.

James, Janet Wilson, ed. *Women in American Religion.* Philadelphia: University of Pennsylvania Press, 1980.

Karlsen, Carol. *The Devil in the Shape of a Woman: Witchcraft in Colonial New England.* New York: Norton, 1998.

Keller, Rosemary Skinner, and Rosemary Radford Ruether. *Encyclopedia of Women and Religion in North America.* Bloomington: Indiana University Press, 2006.

Keller, Rosemary Skinner, and Rosemary Radford Ruether. *In Our Own Voices: Four Centuries of American Women's Religious Writing.* New York: HarperSanFrancisco, 1995.

Kennelly, Karen, ed. *American Catholic Women: A Historical Exploration.* New York: Macmillan, 1989.

Montgomery, Helen Barrett. *Western Women in Eastern Lands: An Outline Study of Fifty Years of Women's Work in Foreign Missions.* New York: Macmillan, 1910.

Rayaprol, Aparna. *Negotiating Identities: Women in the Indian Diaspora.* New York: Oxford University Press, 1997.

Robert, Dana L. *American Women in Mission: A Social History of Their Thought and Practice.* Macon, Ga.: Mercer University Press, 1996.

Rodriguez, Jeanette. *Our Lady of Guadalupe: Faith and Empowerment among Mexican American Women.* Austin: University of Texas Press, 1994.

Stanton, Elizabeth Cady, ed. *The Woman's Bible 1895–1898.* Reprint, Boston: Northeastern University Press, 1993.

Wessinger, Catherine, ed. *Religious Institutions and Women's Leadership: New Roles Inside the Mainstream.* Columbia: University of South Carolina Press, 1996.

AMERICAN WOMEN'S HISTORY

Cott, Nancy F. *The Bonds of Womanhood: "Woman's Sphere" in New England, 1780–1835.* New Haven: Yale University Press, 1977.

Cott, Nancy F., et al. *Roots of Bitterness: Documents of the Social History of American Women*, 2nd ed. Boston: Northeastern University Press, 1996.

Evans, Sara M. *Born for Liberty: A History of Women in America*. New York: Free Press, 1989.

Ulrich, Laurel Thatcher. *Well-Behaved Women Seldom Make History*. New York: Knopf, 2007.

INDEX

ACKNOWLEDGMENTS

I am grateful to Julia Starkey, Emily Neill, and especially Leeanna Varga for research assistance. A sabbatical from Macalester College and the library resources of Harvard Divinity School enabled me to complete the manuscript. Carolyn De Swarte Gifford and Cynthia Eller provided invaluable assistance. Special thanks also go to Colleen McDannell.

ART CREDITS

Arizona Historical Society: frontis, Figure 12; The Boston Athenaeum: Figure 4; Courtesy of the Chicago Historical Society: cover; Florida State Archives: Figure 7, Figure 11; Courtesy of Hadassah, The Women's Zionist Organization of America, Inc.: Figure 15; International Church of the Foursquare Gospel, Heritage Department: Figure 8; The Library Company of Philadelphia: Figure 3; Library of Congress: Figure 2, Figure 6; National Japanese-American Historical Society: Figure 10; Courtesy New York Public Library: Figure 1 (Rare Books Division, Astor, Lenox and Tilden Foundations); The Schlesinger Library, Radcliffe College: Figure 14; The UT Institute of Texan Cultures at San Antonio: Figure 13; Western History Collections, University of Oklahoma: Figure 5; The Western Reserve Historical Society, Cleveland, Ohio: Figure 9.

TEXT CREDITS

"In Memory of My Dear Grand-Child," p. 20: John Harvard Ellis, ed. *The Works of Anne Bradstreet in Prose and Verse*. Gloucester, Mass.: Peter Smith, 1962, pp. 405–6.

"Nothing Is Impossible with God," pp. 40–41: *The Life and Religious Experience of Jarena Lee*, Philadelphia: Printed and published for the author, 1836. Reprinted in William Andrews, ed. *Sisters of the Spirit*. Bloomington: University of Indiana Press, 1986, pp. 35–36.

"Listen to the Talks of Your Sisters," pp. 80–81: Cherokee Women to Cherokee Council, May 2, 1817, series 1, Andrew Jackson

Presidential Papers. Microfilm reel 22. Library of Congress, Manuscripts Division, Washington, D.C.

"The Chain of Tradition Remains Unbroken," pp. 104–5: Marvin Lowenthal, *Henrietta Szold: Life and Letters*. New York: Viking Press, 1942, pp. 92–93.

"My Body Is My Own Business," pp. 130–1: *Toronto Globe and Mail*, Tuesday, June 29, 1993, p. A26.

ABOUT THE AUTHOR

Ann Braude is Director of the Women's Studies in Religion Program at Harvard Divinity School, and Senior Lecturer in the History of Christianity. She has also served on the faculties at Macalester College and Carleton College, and has held visiting appointments at Princeton University, the University of Capetown, and in Harvard's Faculty of Arts and Sciences. Her book *Radical Spirits: Spiritualism and Women's Rights in Nineteenth-Century America* explores the overlap between the early women's rights movement and Spiritualism. She is co-editor of *Root of Bitterness: Documents of the Social History of American Women* and has written many articles on women in Judaism, Christian Science, and other American religious groups. She is also editor of *Transforming the Faiths of Our Fathers: Women Who Changed American Religion.*